AN HISTORICAL SURVEY
OF LITERARY CROATIAN

Anti Bilicu prijateljski

Toronto 23. 2. 20

Branko Franolic

NEL

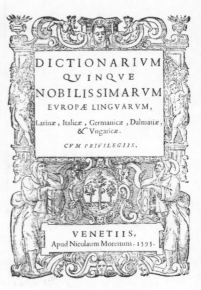

The first page of the Glagolitic Missal (1483)

The title-page of Vrančić's *Dictionarium . . .* (1595)

The title-page of Marulić's *Judita*, 3rd ed. (1522)

The title-page of Kašić's *Institutionum . . .* (1604)

Front cover: The Title-page of the Croatian Missal (Rijeka, 1531)

AN
HISTORICAL SURVEY
OF
LITERARY
CROATIAN

Branko Franolić

Docteur ès Lettres

NOUVELLES EDITIONS LATINES, PARIS

ISBN 2 7233 0126 5

© Branko Franolić, 1984

Nouvelles Editions Latines, 1 Rue Palatine — 75006 Paris

Printed in Great Britain by
Whitstable Litho Ltd., Whitstable, Kent

The Middle Ages

CROATS migrated in the sixth century from White Croatia, a State north of the Carpathians, to the Balkans. When they arrived on the Adriatic coast, settling in more or less the territory they now occupy, they brought with them, and subsequently developed, a palaeo-Croatian language, a branch of Palaeo-Slavonic. This language was divided into a number of dialects, among which the *kaj* dialect predominated in the North, the *ča* dialect in the South (Dalmatia) and part of Bosnia and the *što* dialect in the South East.[1] The dialect boundaries, however, cannot be clearly drawn. There were always areas overlapping isogloss lines between contiguous dialects. Mixed dialects also existed. Owing to the scanty material extant, little can be said with certainty about the linguistic configuration of that part of Europe during this early period.

It is worthy of note that at that time there was little linguistic differentiation in the Slavic world. The differences between the Croatian and the Macedonian dialects, for instance, were no greater than those that exist between British and American English.

Although in the seventh century they were converted to Christianity by priests sent from Rome at the request of the Emperor Heraclius, in the ninth century, the Croats adopted as their liturgical language Old Church Slavonic, based on the Macedonian vernacular of Salonika, which they modified and adapted to their own use for secular purposes and which is today known as Croatian Slavonic or the Croatian version or 'recension' of Old Church Slavonic. Two types of this language, liturgical used in religious services and secular used in non-religious subjects, developed in the late Middle Ages. This religious and secular language, written in Glagolitic characters, survived until the mid-nineteenth century as the literary language of the Glagolitic clergy. This contrasted with the Roman clergy who used the Latin language in the Catholic liturgy[2]. It was still used as a liturgical language in our own times and was replaced by contemporary literary Croatian after the second Vatican Council decision of 1965 that services could be held in the vernacular, and not, as previously, in Latin only. It is therefore this Croatian Slavonic which represents the first Croatian literary language. It became the vehicle of a substantial 'literature'.

The first major text written in Croatian Slavonic is the Baška Tablet of 1100 recording the donation of a site by King Zvonimir to the Benedictine convent of the island of Krk. This document, written in the Glagolitic script, was found in St. Lucy's church near Baška on the island of Krk. It stands as a cornerstone of Croatian literary development although fragments of earlier inscriptions written in the Glagolitic alphabet and dating from the eleventh century have been found on the islands of Krk and Cres (Valun Tablet) and in Istria (Plomin). Fragments of the oldest known Croatian Glagolitic manuscript—*The Glagolita Clozianus* (the beginning of the 11th century)—is a collection of sermons. The codex belonged to the dukes Frankopans from the island of Krk.

Among the oldest documents in the Czech recension of Old Church Slavonic written in Glagolitic are so called *Kiev Folia* named after the place where they are now kept (in the Academy of Science in Kiev). They consist of 17 parchment sheets possibly written in the tenth century in Moravia and contain part of a Greek missal translated into Old Church Slavonic. Parts of the same missal are also contained in the *Vienna Folia* which were written in Croatia about the end of the eleventh century. In the opinion of experts, the *Vienna Folia* are the oldest preserved Glagolitic document with unmistakably Croatian features. There are two parchment sheets with the text in Old Church Slavonic. Under the text there are traces of an older text in Old Church Slavonic but unfortunately the older text of this Glagolitic palimpsest cannot be read. The *Vienna Folia* are also the oldest testimony of the first contacts between Croatian Glagolitic and Czech mediaeval literature. These contacts developed particularly in the 14th century when Croatian Benedictines were invited by Charles IV of Bohemia to Emmaus Monastery in Prague (1347) 'to teach the Church Slavonic language and Glagolitic script'.

Compared to Old Church Slavonic, Croatian Slavonic is a Common Slavonic influenced by Croatian vernacular in the fields of phonetics, morphology and syntax, and, above all, of vocabulary. This hybrid language which was semi-artificial in comparison with the language of the people, was used in notarial acts (in the Church), and in Glagolitic literature, which was, moreover, rich in an age when the number of literate Europeans was small[3]. But very few texts written at that time had an exclusively aesthetic function. The great majority are of a religious character, liturgical or devotional.

After the schism between the Eastern (Orthodox) and Western (Roman) Christian churches in 1054 and the beginning of the Crusades, the Church Slavonic language fell out of use in all West Slavic countries. The only exception was the renaissance of Croatian Church Slavonic in the thirteenth century. In the late Middle Ages, within the framework of the Croatian State, an important technical literature appeared in juridical texts, charters and treaties, beside which flourished a literature of translations of biblical stories, legends, apocrypha, hagiographies and Western mediaeval romances written in Croatian Slavonic. Among other works, the Chronicle of the Priest of Dioclea written about 1149, is outstanding.

It may be assumed that in parallel with this language there existed in the fourteenth and fifteenth centuries a popular literary language (vernacular) used in traditional oral folk poetry and in the poetry created by laymen for use in the afternoon office of the Church, the so-called "prose" for the divine worship. Unlettered people were not hindered in the creation of stories and fables, poetry, drama, or oratory. The first testimony of early Croatian dramatic performance, which is fully credited by scholars, tells of the reception of Pope Alexander III in Zadar in 1117, when the clergy and crowds of people gave recitations of chants in their native language

7

(. . . *cum immensis laudibus et canticis altisone resonantibus in eorum sclavica lingua* . . .). But from the twelfth century the national language, vernacular Croatian, was widely used for inscriptions, legal documents and digests of law, such as in 1189 *Isprava Kulina Bana* (the trade treaty between Dubrovnik and ban Kulin of Bosnia), *Istarski Razvod* (1275) (a record of a survey of the lands of Istria) and in 1288 *Vinodolski Zakonik* (the Statute of Vinodol)[4].

The poets who versified subjects for Church use seem to have been called *začinjavci* "chanters"[5]. They, and other literary men, particularly translators, scribes, copyists and compilers, gradually introduced the vernacular into the literary field. They were the precursors of the rich poetic literature in the Croat language that appeared in the fifteenth and sixteenth centuries.

One of the oldest recorded Croatian poems is the 14th century *Cantilena pro sabatho* (1385) by an unknown author but transcribed by the Franciscan Paulus de Sclavonia (de Sebenico) who also recorded the *Šibenik Prayer* (*Šibenska molitva*), ca. 1347. *Cantilena* contains 132 evenly rhymed octosyllables and relates the events of Good Friday and Saturday. The poem is preserved in the 14th century Latin Codex kept in Budapest library Szecheneyi.

With the appearance of literary works destined for lay readers, resulting from the growing contact with Western literatures, the native vernacular gradually penetrated the literary language. The current daily language appeared more and more frequently in the translations of chivalresque romances like those of Troy (ca. 1300) and Alexander the Great, of spiritual lyrics such as the fifteenth-century *Torments of Jesus* and, above all, in mediaeval mystery and miracle plays[6]. This leads M. Kombol to say that: "In this way the transformation occurred in Croatian literature as early as the Middle Ages which occurred in Russian literature in the time of Peter the Great (1680—1725) and in Serbian and Bulgarian literature in the nineteenth century; that is to say, in Croatian literature the vernacular already predominated at that date."
(cf. M. Kombol, *Povijest hrvatske književnosti do narodnog*

preporoda, History of Croatian Literature up to the National Revival, 1945, p. 22). "The *lingua vernacula* secured a place of its own very early, so that when we assess Croatian mediaeval literature as democratic and national, this is above all so on account of its language and only later—or parallel with it because of its thematic orientation." (E. Hercigonja, *The Place and Role of Croatian Literature in the Literary Development of the Slavonic Middle Ages,* in *Comparative Studies in Croatian Literature,* Zagreb, 1981, 30.)

Baščanska ploča (The Baška Tablet; c. 1100)

The Renaissance

The use of the vernacular in literary language was accelerated by the appearance of national literature written in the local dialects of the cities of Dubrovnik, Split, Zadar and Hvar. In these cities, Glagolitic literature formed the basis upon which a new Croatian literary movement could develop, relying heavily on the native urban civilization based largely on trade.[7] Amongst Slavic literatures the Renaissance appeared most clearly in Croatian and Polish. The Croatian Renaissance in Dalmatia was linked primarily with urban culture. Enjoying relative security and protected from Turkish incursions by the mountains in the background, the cities of the Dalmatian Littoral were open to western, and especially Italian, influences, since a great number of young people were sent to study at the Italian universities such as Padua and Bologna. In these Dalmatian cities, beside the numerous Humanists who wrote in Latin, poets influenced by the Italian Renaissance and writing in Croat began to assert themselves. They produced lyric poetry, eclogues, pastoral dramas and novels, comedies, masques, and other Renaissance literary genres and gave Croat literature a secular character. As a result, the range of literature broadened considerably. There was no unique and standard literary language prevailing at that time, since every writer used his local vernacular, in which Romance (Dalmatian) borrowings were numerous, yet ties between the various areas were close and tendencies toward normalization clearly existed.

The extinct Romance language Dalmatian was at that time still spoken in relatively small communities on the eastern shores of the Adriatic, whence the name Dalmatian. Its two recorded dialects were *Vegliot*, spoken on the island of Krk (Veglia), which became extinct with the death of Antun (Tone)

Udina in 1898 and *Ragusan* (Dubrovnik), known only from documents dating from the 13th to the 16th centuries. Beside many toponyms, there are several Dalmatian lexical remnants to be found in contemporary Croat, e.g. *jarbol* 'mast', *korizma* 'Lent', *komostre* 'pothanger, pothook', *murva* 'mulberry', *pršutak* 'prosciutto—raw ham', *dupin* 'dolphin', *jegulja* 'eel', *jastog* 'lobster', *liganj* 'squid', *mušalj* 'mussel', *sipa* 'cuttle fish', *štriga* 'a witch', and the names of many fish: *raža, salpa, skarpina, gira, kijerna, kantar/-or*, etc.[8]

Parallel to this phenomenon, the Latin alphabet spread more and more and, as the public use of the Glagolitic script diminished, finally became the alphabet commonly accepted by the Croats[9], while from the fourteenth century Latin was increasingly used. The universality of Latin in Western Europe was due to the fact that it was the only language of culture far into the Middle Ages and witness to antiquity. Latin had the qualities of elegance and stability that Croat seemed to lack. The neo-Latin poetry of Croat writers was important to European literature as a whole and was exemplified in the writings of Janus Pannonius (Ivan Česmički [1434-72]), Aelius Lampridius Cerva (Ilija Crijević [1463-1520]) and Marko Marulić (1450-1524). As in Italy, neo-Latin prose and poetry constituted for Croat writers and poets a basis for the subsequent development of the norms of the national literary language and new poetic genres. Throughout the late Middle Ages there remained a strong rivalry with Latin, and Croat had to prove itself as a language of culture. It had to show that it was capable of conveying general ideas and shades of meaning in an abstract vocabulary. The work of the sixteenth-century Humanists and Renaissance poets was fundamental to this. For them, all means were good to enrich the language: neologisms, borrowings, Latin and Italian calques, archaisms, regionalisms. Finnish scholar Jukka Hyrkkänen, in his outstanding study *Der Lexicalische Einfluss des Italienischen auf das Kroatische des 16. Jahrhunderts*, records over one thousand Italian lexical borrowings in the 16th century literary Croatian.[10]

However, it was commonly felt that the Croat language was

not fit to bear comparison with the major languages of Western Europe, such as Italian. Thus the Croat Petrarchists of Renaissance Dalmatia made a distinctive contribution to European Petrarchism through the poetry of Sabo Bobaljević Mišetić, Domenico Ragnina (Dinko Ranjina), Georgio Bizanti, Lodovico Paschale (Paskalić) and Miho Monaldi, who wrote largely, if not exclusively, in Italian. Directly or indirectly those Dalmatian Petrarchists appear to have had some influence on French and English sonneteers, including Shakespeare. One may justly say that the Dalmatian poets could 'expand' a little when they chose and make a contribution to the Petrarchism of Europe.[11] Although cosmopolitan in form, 15th and 16th century Croatian Humanism reflected a certain individuality in its content and feeling that was rooted in its native soil and developed into the special conditions of Croatian historical cultural development. More important than the question of cosmopolitism versus patriotism is the fact that these Humanists represented a considerable advance in the Croatian literature. Regarding sixteenth-century literary activity in Dalmatia and Dubrovnik, which flourished in three languages (i.e. Latin, Italian, and Croatian), Riccardo Picchio thinks that "in many instances we should speak of a common area of civilization including both Italy and a significant part of the Croatian lands rather than of influence or typological equivalences. ... The disputes regarding the appropriateness of a Croatian vernacular to perform the functions of a literary language depended, therefore, on answering the basic question of whether this Croatian vernacular was qualified for literary 'imitation' of Latin and/or Italian models".[12]

Versification[13] in the vernacular had existed since the fourteenth century, although the first major poet is considered to be Marko Marulić (1450-1524) from Split, whose poem *Judita* (*Istoria svete udovice Judit u versih hrvacki složena*, i.e. "The history of the holy widow Judith, written in Croatian verses"), first published in Venice in 1521, includes an introduction dated 1501. Let us note that the first Croatian books printed in Latin script or in Glagolitic were published in Venice, which had become, after the invention of printing, the major centre of the new art. Thus the first Croatian Glagolitic primer (*bukvar*), the *Introductorium Croatice*, was also published in Venice in 1527; it is a small book, interesting not only for its beautifully illustrated sections, but also for its contents— including an alphabet and a section on grammar. The first Croat book ever to be printed had actually been published thirty-eight years before *Judita*. It was a Glagolitic missal in folio from 1483. The earliest extant Croatian lectionary, printed in Gothic characters in Venice (1495) is the *Lectionarium* of Father Bernardinus from Split. It is written in a language very similar to that of Marulić. Marulić wrote in *ča* dialect, but sometimes using *što* forms to facilitate the difficult rhyme pattern. Since "Judith" was the first work of broader conception dominated by a consciously patriotic idea, Marulić was generally regarded as the founder of Croatian poetic art. It is for this reason that he has retained this title of honour to the present day, although he was chronologically preceded by the oldest of the known and unknown Petrarchan poets of Ragusa (Dubrovnik), who were among the founding fathers of Croatian literature.

At the same time, at the end of the fifteenth and beginning of the sixteenth centuries the first Petrarchists of the Renaissance appeared at Dubrovnik. Imbued with humanistic spirit and nourished with folk poetry, they formed an inexhaustible source of genuine language of poetical inspiration. They felt that Croat needed to be strengthened from its own resources. In fact, "in creating a lyrical medium, they found inspiration in folk poetry and also used the linguistic experience of church and religious literature in general".[14] The first generation of these poets, Šiško Menčetić Vlahović (1457-1527), Džore Držić (1461-1501), Marin Krističević (died in 1531) and others, wrote in Ragusan *ča* dialect, later replaced by Ragusan *što* dialect among the sixteenth and seventeenth-century writers such as Marin Držić, Gundulić, Bunić and Palmotić, who wrote in the *što-(i)je* dialect. It was under the influence of the spoken *što-(i)je* dialect of neighbouring Herzegovina that Ragusan literary language, with its *ča* sub-

13

stratum[15], turned increasingly towards *što* to reach in the seventeenth century an elaborate expression of the *što* literary language.

From the middle of the sixteenth to the end of the seventeenth century the Dubrovnik Republic was the most important cultural and scientific centre in the Balkans. It was "the Croatian Athens", or "the crown of all Croatian cities" as the poet Ivan Vidali, from the island of Korčula, called it in 1564 in a poetic epistle addressed to his fellow-poet Nikola Nalješković in Dubrovnik.

While a Croatian literary language was being born in the little republic of Ragusa, a Croatian literature in the *ča* dialect was being created simultaneously around the towns of Split, Zadar, and the Island of Hvar. It was the writers who succeeded Marulić, namely Hanibal Lucić, Petar Hektorović, Mikša Pelegrinović, Martin Benetović of Hvar and Petar Zoranić, Šime Budinić, Brne Krnarutić and Juraj Baraković of Zadar who wrote in the *ča* dialect. "Their language shows local differences, and even the influence of the štokavic dialect. Normalizing factors existed in the form of the influence of the štokavic dialect of neighbouring Dubrovnik and in the continuing tradition of the mediaeval Glagolitic literature".[16] It should be noted that in his epic poem *Vazetje Sigeta grada* (*The Capture of the City of Sziget*, 1584), Krnarutić consciously aimed at creating a Croatian literary koiné by freely mixing *ča, što* and *kaj* dialects, while Aleksandar Komulović from Split, the author of *Nauk krstjanski za slovinski narod*, printed in Rome (1582), also used many *što* forms in his writings and held views similar to those of Bartol Kašić. This first Croatian Pan-Slavist made two trips to Moscow (1595-97) but returned bitterly disappointed. "To please the Russians he also introduced Russianisms into his Croatian writing."

In Budinić's *Pokorni psalmi Davidovi* (*Penitential Psalms of David*, Venice 1582), we encounter the first effort to introduce diacritic signs into the Croatian alphabet. Generally speaking the Slavic languages written in Roman script (Croatian, Czech, Slovak, Slovene, Lusatian and Polish) have to use a large number of diacritical marks (*č, ć, š, ž,* etc.) because so many specifically Slavic sounds have no equivalent Roman letter. In the 16th century, Croatian spelling varied a good deal from writer to writer, and even within the work of a single writer. But there were forces, like printing, making for standardization, and there were a good many generally accepted spelling-conventions. For example, *u* and *v* could both be used for the consonant or for the vowel, and it was normal to use *v* at the beginning of a word (*vzrok, vnuk*) and *u* elsewhere (*kruh, kuga, lupes*).[17] In Northern Croatia Hungarian orthography was used whereas in Dalmatia Italian. Standardization did not take place until the 19th century, and the spellings then established were on the whole the ones the Croatians still use.

It was in the sixteenth century that *ča* literature reached its golden age in a literary blossoming which covered the whole east Adriatic coast from the peninsula of Istria in the North to the Bay of Kotor in the South. The čakavic literary dialect of Dalmatia fell into disuse after the seventeenth century.

The prestige of the čakavic dialect of Dalmatia was so widespread that Faust Vrančić (Faustus Verantius) in his *Dictionarium quinque nobilissimarum Europae linguarum* (Venice, 1595) ranks Croatian alongside Latin, Italian, German, and Hungarian, as the five noblest languages of Europe. However, the Ragusan poet Dominko Zlatarić (1558-1610), who translated Sophocles' tragedy *Electra*, Tasso's pastoral drama *Aminta* and Love and Death of Pyramus and Thisbe, a paraphrase of Ovid's metamorphosis, was aware that he had translated these works "from major foreign languages into Croatian" (*iz veće tuđieh jezika u hrvacki izložene*) as is written on the title-page of his *Elektra*, printed in Venice in 1597.

The title-page of Zlatarić's translation of *Electra* (1597)

The Reformation

The Reformation, and the loosening of the ties of a centralized Church organization in Europe led to men abandoning Latin as a normal means of communication in speech or writing. In Croatia the Reformation continued the long Glagolitic literary tradition.

The 16th century Protestant writers and translators of religious books, Stjepan Konzul Istranin (1521-68), Anton Dalmatin, Juraj Cvečić, etc., wrote in the *ča* dialect of Istria and the Croatian Littoral. The most significant Croatian Protestant book "Conversation Between a Papist and a Lutheran" published in 1555 (in Tübingen), was written in the čakavic dialect of Istria by the eminent theological controversialist Matthias Flacius Illyricus (1520-1575) from Labin in Istria. In order that their books might be read by the speakers of the other dialects, these writers tried, by merging the dialects, to create a written language easily understandable to all Croats and South Slavs. They expounded the theoretical justification for such a fusion of dialects in the preface to the Glagolitic edition of the *New Testament, Part one*, edited in Tübingen in 1562. To flee from the Inquisition, the most prominent Protestants from Istria and the adjacent Croatian Littoral emigrated to Germany. Among the emigrants were Stjepan Konzul Istranin, Matija Živić, Juraj Cvečić from Pazin, Lav Marčetić from Rijeka, Juraj Jurčić from Vinodol, Antun Bočić from Modruš, Anton Dalmatin from Senj and many others. Following Martin Luther's dictum: "Whatever I learnt, I preached and whatever I preached, I printed", the Croatian Protestant writers developed a great printing activity, which made possible a speedy diffusion of their doctrine. In about 1560, with the help of the reigning Duke of Württemberg, Christoph, they established, in his castle of

Amandenhof, near Urah and Tübingen, a Croatian printing press. From 1561 to 1565 up to twenty-five different Croatian Protestant books—in editions of 25,000 copies each—were printed there in Glagolitic, Latin and Bosnian (Western) Cyrillic scripts, for use in South-Slav countries. Only about 300 copies are now extant, most of them preserved in German libraries. Stjepan Konzul from Istria and Anton Dalmatin from the town of Senj on the Croatian Littoral wrote together in a Protestant publication: "God has sent us to Germany and made us learn His divine truth through papal persecution; having found it, we shall spread it in Croatian among many nations, so that those not knowing it shall know it". In their translations, mostly from German, of different evangelical books, they showed considerable skill in adapting the vernacular to the complex needs of precise literary expression.[18] They always referred to their language as 'Croatian' and insisted on scrupulous observance of purity in the language and style.[19]

During the Renaissance and the Reformation Croatian acquired such prestige among Slavonic languages that Polish cardinal Stanislaus Hosius (1504-1579), one of the most significant figures of the Counter-Reformation, wrote: *"Quamlibet autem non ipsos amemus, tamen illud fateamur necesse est: Sclavorum aut Dalmatarum linguam esse multo elegantiorem quam sit nostra, ita, ut si precationes & sacras lectiones in vernaculam transferri linguam oporteret, in eam potissimum transferendae sint a qua nostra duxit originem, quae praestat etiam caeteris elegantia. Cum praesertim Dalmatica lingua sacros libros Hieronymum vertisse constet, ut in eius usu minus esse periculi videatur."* (*Dialogus De Eo, num calicem laicis et uxores sacerdotibus permitti, ac divina officia vulgari lingua peragi fas sit.* Dilinge, 1558.)

It is evident that Hosius accepted the legend that St. Jerome, a native of Dalmatia, had invented the Glagolitic alphabet and that he had translated the Holy Scriptures not only into Latin but also into the Slavic language of his countrymen. This legend was so widely accepted that it helped preserve the Slavonic language and Glagolitic liturgy in the Croatian lands.

The impact of Croatian Protestant writings and literary

language was possible only through the medium of the lately invented printing press. Without the press the success of the Reformation in Croatia would certainly have been much more limited. Granted, at the time of the Reformation not even five per cent of the people read.

In Nedelišće, a market town of Medjumurje, Count Juraj Zrinjski founded a printing office in 1570 where two Croatian Protestant books were printed: Mihajlo Bučić's *Novi Zavjet* (The New Testament) and *Katekizam* (Catechism). There was also printed in 1574 the translation of István Verböczy's book *Decretum Tripartitum* in the old kajkavic dialect. This translation is the first attempt to use the kajkavic dialect as a literary medium. Thus in the sixteenth century the *kaj* dialect also appeared on the Croatian literary scene. It was used by the writers of North Croatia whose capital was the city of Zagreb. The pioneers and standard bearers of this *kaj* literary language were the Zagreb canon Antun Vramec whose works *Kronika* and *Postila* were printed in Ljubljana (1578) and Varaždin (1586) respectively, and the town notary in Varaždin Ivan Pergošić whose translation of the Common Law manual *Decretum Tripartitum* was published in 1574[20]. Pergošić translated some portions of the codex into štokavic, a fact which points to the need that even the first kajkavic writers felt to break free of the narrow limitations of their own dialect.

The kajkavic dialect also showed some degree of štokavic influence and in the second half of the eighteenth century had developed into a relatively normalized form, as in the plays of Tituš Brezovački. The differences between the literary dialects were never, however, clear-cut. Writers were reasonably aware of the kind of language used in the other areas, and the language of some writers was a hybrid of more than one dialect. Such has been the case, for example, with the seventeenth century writers in Northern Croatia, Petar Zrinjski and Pavao Ritter-Vitezović. They both freely mix the čakavic and kajkavic dialects; but while in Zrinjski the mixture is casual, Vitezović consciously aimed at blending three dialects for the purpose of creating a common Croatian literary language. Vitezović's effort anticipated by more than a century

18

the "Illyrian Awakening" from which would finally emerge a unified Croatian literary language.

The title-page of Vramec's *Kronika* (1578)

The Seventeenth Century

Nevertheless at this time convergent tendencies toward unity and normalization clearly existed. It was already accepted that the *što* dialect should form the basis of the standard literary language, and this idea stimulated many of the Croats of these early centuries in their literary creation. Although in 1604 Bartol Kašić (1575-1650) of the Island of Pag wrote in Latin a grammar of the *ča-i* and *što-i* dialects (*Institutiones linguae illyricae libri duo*), he nevertheless chose the *što-i* dialect for his translation of the Bible in 1622. He urged the reformation of orthography and demanded that the somewhat stylized poetic language be brought closer to that of the people. In his view the finest Croatian language was that based on *što*. In the preface to his Croat translation of *Roman Ritual* (Rome, 1640), Kašić declares that the štokavic-ikavic dialect of Bosnia is "the most common, and that everyone can understand it" and for that reason he proposes it as the common national language. He also proposes the reform of Croatian spelling, suggesting that every letter should consistently represent the same single phoneme. This spelling reform, based on a sound-for-symbol correspondence, was expounded by the Benedictine, Raymond Giamagnich, in his booklet *Nauk za pisati dobro latinskiema slovima rieci yezika slovinskoga...* (Principles for Writing Properly, in Roman Characters, the Words of the Croatian Language), published in Venice in 1639 by Marco Ginammi. Giamagnich's booklet "proposes a logical orthographic (spelling) and phonetic system, some two hundred years before Vuk Karadžić and Ljudevit Gaj"[21]. In his *Aus der Geschichte der lateinischen Schrift bei den Südslaven*, Bayerische Akademie der Wissenschaften, Philosophisch-historische Klasse, 1950 Heft 10, pp. 13, 14, P. Diels showed that it was necessary, at that time, to invent a special spelling system for k, g, s, z, š, ž, c, ć, đ, č (dž), j, ļ, ń and dz. "This is exactly what Giamagnich had done".[22]

The Jesuit Jacobo Micaglia also proclaimed in the preface to his *Dictionary* and *Latin Grammar* (1649-51) that "la lingua bosnese (i.e. Ragusan *što* dialect) è la più bella". The fact that the language of the Ragusan poet Junije Palmotić (1607-1657) turned towards *što* must also be attributed to this same Kašić.

This predilection for the *što-(i)je* dialect is explained by the influence which may have been exercised over the Croatians by Ragusan literature in the *što-(i)je* dialect from the fifteenth to the eighteenth centuries. Thus, under the influence of Ragusan literature, seventeenth-century writers in Dalmatia, such as Ivanišević, Kanavelović, Kavanjin, Vitaljić and Tanclinger-Zanotti, turned increasingly towards *što* dialect. The štokavic dialect also became the literary language in Bosnia used by the seventeenth-century Franciscans M. Divković (1563-1631), S. Matijević, P. Posilović (died in 1651), P. Papić, I. Bandulavić and I. Ančić. For these writers and their epoch the function of literature was to "instruct and delight" as dictated by Horace and encouraged by both Catholicism and the Counter-Reformation.

THE IMPACT OF THE COUNTER-REFORMATION

During the Counter-Reformation period, both in Bosnia and Croatia (Slavonia and Dalmatia) the moral responsibilities and qualities of literature are repeatedly stressed either in the works of fiction themselves or in the numerous didactico-religious works which were being published. Concerned to stop the spread of Protestantism in Croatia and of Islam in Bosnia, the Catholic religious orders were, moreover, aware that literature was reaching a wider public and they realised its edifying potentialities. Guided by the work of Jesuits both at home and abroad, literary creation expressed broad doctrines advocating unification of the South Slavs and reunion of the Eastern Christians with Rome.

The Counter-Reformation made use of the medium that

the Protestants, continuing the long Glagolitic tradition of Istria and the Croatian Littoral, first used, namely the native language or the vernacular. The Church continued the use of Latin for a great number of reasons; its witness to antiquity, its universality, the sacred music composed for religious texts in Latin and its faithfulness as a language of worship. Yet with changing cultures, there was a widespread desire for the vernacular to be used. This was encouraged by the Congregation for the Propagation of the Faith (*Congregatio de Propaganda Fide*). Thus the Jesuit Bartol Kašić, commissioned by the Jesuit father general Claude Acquaviva, prepared the grammar *Institutiones...* in 1604 for the Croatian students at the *Academia Linguae Illyricae* in Rome. It was an attempt to describe the grammar of Croat in terms of the grammar of Latin: Croat was said to have a distinct ablative case, gerundive, subjunctive mood, and so forth; so that a knowledge of Latin was necessary either to read the grammar or to share in its assumptions. Nevertheless, in this first Croatian grammar, Kašić indicated with proper precision the accentuation of Croatian words.[23] Nor were the earliest dictionaries of Croat much better; in the sixteenth and seventeenth centuries, they were bilingual or multilingual lists of words. They made scant attempt to record and analyse Croat in its own right. In the mid-seventeenth century the Jesuit Jacobo Micaglia compiled a Croatian-Italian-Latin dictionary, *Blago jezika Slovinskoga* (1649), a "Treasury of the Illyric Language", published at Loretto-Ancona at the expense of the Congregation. This dictionary, designed for "the children of Dalmatia", contains words taken from *što-i* and *ča* dialects. By the end of the century another trilingual dictionary, *Vocabolario di tre nobilissimi linguaggi: italiano, illirico e latino* (1679), was compiled by the purist lexicographer Ivan Tanclinger-Zanotti from Zadar. It is worth noting that whereas Protestant writers called their language only 'Croatian', Counter-Reformation writers called it 'Croatian', *'Slovinski'* or 'Illyrian'.[23a]

The Counter-Reformation aimed to reach all Croat territories and social ranks. To achieve this purpose the monks and missionaries had to address the ordinary people in their own vernacular rather than Latin. Therefore in Northern Croatia in the seventeenth century there was a striking increase in the number of popular religious poems based on secular lyrics, intended as a substitute for profane love poems. To facilitate the substitution, the poems are set to the music of folk songs. These religious poems are excellent original sources for tracing the flowering of folk poetry in the kajkavic territory even prior to the Reformation.

At the same time Bosnian Franciscans re-edited the old Croat Glagolitic missals, introducing into them the elements of the *što* vernacular spoken in Bosnia. But more important were their catechisms, prayer books and Christian inspirational works, almost all of them translations or adaptations in Croatian of Latin or Italian works or compilations of works of Croatian writers from Dalmatia and Dubrovnik. These works of the Franciscans are of great philological interest and value. They are written in the štokavic dialect and thus contributed to the dissemination of this dialect which two centuries later would be adopted as the literary language by other Croatian regions. The didactic purpose of such devotional writing was obvious. From a literary point of view most of this writing is mediocre, but it nevertheless performed an important spiritual function and formed a living tradition which a serious poet could exploit. The distinctive feature of this didactico-religious literature is the conscientious effort of the writers to build up a common standard *što* language which could gain supremacy over the other dialects and be accepted as the most proper form of literary Croatian by the speakers of different dialects. This was, indeed, an outcome of the activity carried on by the Counter-Reformation, although this tendency toward a common litarary language did not emerge fully until the nineteenth century.

As a result of Counter-Reformation activity the Catholic Church had unwittingly laid the foundation for the Croat national revival by emphasizing the vernacular tongue in worship and by allowing clerics to publish regularly in the Croatian language.[24]

The Eighteenth Century

The štokavic literature of the seventeenth century written by Catholic religious (Franciscans and Jesuits) of Bosnia and Dalmatia was the source of the eighteenth century rebirth of Croatian literature and language which reaches its zenith in the works of the two Dalmatian Franciscans, Filip Grabovac (1697-1749) and Andrija Kačić Miošić (1704-1760), the forerunners of modern Croatian nationalism. Grabovac's work *The Flower of Conversation of the Illyrian or Croatian People and Language* (Venice, 1747) was seized by Venetian authorities and its author, imprisoned in Venice, died as a martyr of the national idea. His successor, A. Kačić-Miošić, under the influence of the Enlightenment compiled his famous collection of prose and poetry entitled *Razgovor ugodni naroda Slovinskoga* (The Pleasant Discourse of the Slav People) which was published in Venice in 1756. Written in an extremely simple style, in a popular way, "for labourers and shepherds", it had a great influence at all levels of society and despite its obvious literary defects it became a folk patriotic catechism.[25]

The *što-i* dialect also spread as a literary language in Slavonia (now North-East Croatia) and was used by the writers Antun Kanižlić (1699-1777), Matija Antun Reljković (1732-1798), one of the first representatives of the Enlightenment in Croatia, and the learned Franciscan Petar Katančić (1750-1825), the author of the first Croatian, unpublished, etymological dictionary *Etymologicon Illyricum* (1473 pp.). Katančić thought that Bosnian (*što*) dialect was the most beautiful (*"Bosnenses puritate atque elegantia eminent"*) and translated the Bible into this dialect.[26]

By about the middle of the eighteenth century the great majority of Croatian writers were using the *što* language. The *kaj* tradition continued only in and around Zagreb, while

24

everywhere else in Bosnia, Herzegovina, Slavonia and Dalmatia writers used the *što* dialect.[27] This mid-eighteenth century neo-štokavic language marks the real beginning of contemporary Standard Croatian.[28]

In this way between the fifteenth and the eighteenth centuries the *što-i* or *što-je* dialect conquered the greater part of Croatian territory. The result was the appearance of *što* dictionaries and grammars; the *Dizionario Italiano-Latino-Illirico* of the Jesuit A. Della Bella (in Ragusan with quotations from Dalmatian writers, published in Venice in 1728, reprinted in Dubrovnik in 1785); *Grammatica della lingua illirica* of 1808 by F.M. Appendini which was also in *-ije* Ragusan, as well as the 6 volume Latin-Italian-Croat dictionary of 4721 pages by the Franciscan Joachim Stulli (compiled in 1782, but published only in 1801 (first part) in Buda, 1806 (second part) and 1810 (third part) in Dubrovnik). The second part of Stulli's dictionary (*Rječjosložje*) contains 80,000 entries.[29] Similar manuals appeared in Bosnia, Slavonia and Italy, all in *što*.[30]

Similarly, the *kaj* dialect writers and lexicographers of the age (Belostenec, Vitezović in the seventeenth century, and Jambrešić and Patačić in the eighteenth) defended the idea of the common *što-(i)je* language. Special mention must be made of *Gazophylacium seu latino-illyricorum onomatum aerarium* (Zagreb, 1740) 1962 pages in -4° by I. Belostenec (1595-1675), which is effectively the first encyclopedic dictionary of the Croatian language. This work, written in the seventeenth century and printed in the eighteenth, is the largest and richest dictionary of this period in the *kaj* dialect. No Croatian writer or lexicographer has embodied in his writing so many *kaj, ča* and *što* elements and terms as Belostenec in his *Gazophylacium*. As a Paulist and Prior of his order, he stayed in the different regions and learnt all the Croatian dialects. In this way he drew upon the different forms of the local languages to compile the wealth of lexical treasure in his dictionary. In the dictionary itself the dialectal terms are found side by side, and this is expressly indicated. Belostenec's dictionary rightly had enormous influence and its publication was the most important linguistic event of the eighteenth century.

By the same token the *Lexicon Latino-Illyricum* of 1708 by Pavao Ritter Vitezović (1652-1713), which is preserved in 1132 quarto pages of manuscript, introduces the terms of the three Croatian dialects. For each Latin term Vitezović gave the semantic equivalent from all the basic dialects. For example, the Latin word *quidquid* is translated by the following words: *čagod, štogod, kajgod, štogodar, štogodir*; and Latin *quid* by *ča, kaj, što, čto;* Latin *narrare* by: *praviti, kazati, povedat, kazivati.* His Latin-Illyrian dictionary shows that he had in mind a linguistic unity without confining himself to any particular dialect or specific speech-forms. This great innovator also attempted, after Budinić and Kašić, a reform of Croatian Latin spelling and script. The fundamental principle of this reform, which was later to be elaborated and applied by Ljudevit Gaj, is that a single letter (grapheme) must correspond to each sound (phoneme). By rejecting digraphs and introducing diacritic marks he made it possible to write in one letter a sound that had formerly been written in two or more (such as *č* instead of the former *cs*, etc.). Like Vitezović, the Jesuit Andrija Jambrešić (1700-1758) also proposed a spelling reform of kajkavic Croatian in his *Manuductio ad croaticam orthographiam* (Zagreb, 1732) by using diacritic signs. By virtue of his literary, historical and philological work, Vitezović is regarded as the forerunner of Ljudevit Gaj (1809-1871) and of the Croatian literary and national revival at the beginning of the nineteenth century.

During the Napoleonic occupation, a Croatian-French grammar (*Nova Ričoslovnica iliričko-franceska*) by Šime Starčević and a Croatian grammar (*Nova ričoslovnica ilirička*) by the same author, were written in *što-i* dialect and published in 1812 in Trieste. In his Illyrian grammar Starčević was the first to attempt a description of the *neo-što* accentual system.[31] The functional approach and accuracy of this first description of suprasegmental features in neo-štokavic has been somewhat overlooked and the value of Starčević's grammar from the phonological point of view has not been sufficiently stressed in pre-war Yugoslavia. Prague phonologists used the material provided by Starčević abundantly when outlining principles of the suprasegmental features of South Slav speeches. Further, both N.S. Trubezkoy in his *Principes de Phonologie* (Paris 1957, p. 211, 227-228) and R. Jakobson in *Die Betonung und ihre Rolle in der Wort- und Syntagmaphonologie* (T.C. L.P. 4. p. 164 & seq.) refer to Starčević.

From all this it can be concluded that Croatian literature written in the *što* dialect goes back to the fifteenth century and continues down to the nineteenth century, steadily spreading and finally prevailing over the other two dialect literatures (*ča* and *kaj*).

Nevertheless even in our own day *ča* and *kaj* literatures are living and productive, although relegated to the background. Many twentieth-century poets wrote either in *kaj* (A.G. Matoš, D. Domjanić, F. Galović, I. Goran Kovačić, M. Krleža, M. Pavlek Miškina, S. Kolar, N. Pavić, T. Prpić) or in *ča* (V. Nazor, M. Balota, D. Gervais, A. Cettineo, M. Franičević, Z. Črnja, D. Ivanišević, N. Bonifačić-Rožin, P. Ljubić, M. Uvodić). In the '30s there was a considerable renewal and expansion of dialect poetry. After the Second World War and again even more recently there has been a revival of these regional literatures and a host of young poets started to write in *kaj* or *ča* dialects.[32] Moreover, poets who come neither from Bosnia or Herzegovina nor from Slavonia or North Dalmatia feel much more at ease when writing in their regional speech, which gives their poetry special charm and local colour. It is an intimate language, a folk-language, the language of a closely-knit community in which every word seems to have overtones, a flavour. As these writers sometimes write indiscriminately in *što*, *ča* or *kaj* there are a number of cross-influences between the different dialects both in grammar and vocabulary. They enrich the general vocabulary of the standard literary language by providing a regional lexical contribution, introducing into *što* literature words and phraseology peculiar to the regions.

Modern literary Croatian is a final conquest over dialect, since the influence of the substratum (*kaj* or *ča*) on the *što*

27

dialect is very considerable in variations of accent and of vocabulary. Moreover, the Croats are inexhaustible on questions of philology, on the different dialects and on the propriety of turns of phrase and terms in good *što*. This koine, often learnt at school, and menaced by dialectal pronunciations and turns of speech (*ča* and *kaj*), is treated with all the laborious care of which its construction is worthy.

Among the Croats, their literary tradition exercised a great influence on the formation of the standard language in the nineteenth century and its evolution in the twentieth. The feeling of historical continuity and of the links with the writers of the fifteenth and sixteenth centuries is obvious among contemporary writers and there is a clear affiliation between *začinjavci*, Marulić, Kačić, Botić, Kranjčević and Ujević, between Vramec, Brezovački, Đalski, Matoš, Krleža, and Goran Kovačić, or between Držić, Gundulić, Mažuranić, Šenoa, Nazor, Šegedin and Marinković. Whatever changes have taken place in vocabulary or in the elements of grammar with the lapse of time, the fact nevertheless remains that both the litarary languages of the sixteenth and twentieth centuries are Croatian by virtue of the principle of linguistic continuity, since linguistic features are fundamentally traditional in character.[33]   The linguistic comparison of the Lord's Prayer of 1595 with the 1968 version, illustrates the continuity of literary Croatian.

The 1595 version (in modern spelling): *Oče naš koji jesi na nebesih. Sveti se ime tvoje. Pridi kraljevstvo tvoje. Budi volja tvoja. Kako na nebu tako i na zemlji. Kruh naš svagdanji daj nam danas i otpusti nam duge naše, kako i mi otpušćamo dužnikom našim. I ne uvedi nas u napast da oslobodi nas oda zla. Amen.* [The Lord's Prayer from F. Vrančić's *Dictionarium Quinque Nobilissimarum Europae Linguarum*, Venice 1595 p. 127.]

The 1968 version: *Oče naš, koji jesi na nebesima, sveti se ime tvoje, dođi kraljevstvo tvoje, budi volja tvoja kako na nebu tako i na zemlji. Kruh naš svagdanji daj nam danas. I otpusti nam duge naše kako i mi otpuštamo dužnicima našim. I ne uvedi nas u napast, nego izbavi nas od zla.* (The Lord's Prayer from *Rimski Misal*, Kršćanska Sadašnjost, Zagreb 1968, p. 420).

When we observe the development of the written form of the Croatian vernacular between the early sixteenth century to the national revival which began in the late eighteenth century, the tendency seems to have been towards fragmentation. The life of the literary language was polycentric. Yet "there is the consciousness of the fundamental unity of the language. This is expressed in a most striking fashion at the very beginning of the modern period by the use of the term 'Croatian' to describe two very different representatives of the vernacular. Bishop Šimun Kožičić of Modruš entitled his Missal, printed at his house in Rijeka in 1533, *Misal hrvacki* (Croatian Missal), and the term is used by him more than once in describing his six religious publications".[34] It is noteworthy that Kožičić does not call his Missal 'Roman' as was customary at that time, but dedicates it "to glory of God and to the consecration of the Croatian language" (*na Božju hvalu i hrvackoga ezika posvećen'e*), obviously considering that Croatian had legitimate rights as a liturgical language.

"'Croatian' is also the word used by Marko Marulić (from Split) writing only ten years earlier than Bishop Kožičić, to describe his story of Judith. Yet how different is the Spalatine čakavic of the humanist Marulić from the liturgical language of the books of Rijeka! Despite the differences, both forms of the vernacular are felt by their users to be exponents of a single national idiom. Later, in the seventeenth and eighteenth centuries, we find a number of instances of a mixture of dialects, conscious or unconscious." ... "Eighteenth-century grammarians, too, were aware of the essential unity of the 'Illyrian' dialects; even though those who wrote in Dubrovnik may have regarded the Ragusan literary dialect as a kind of *volgare illustre*",[35] as Dante used to call koiné used in Italy by poets, which while borrowing elements from all the dialects, transcends them all.

"A Neo-štokavic literary language shaped on the model of the koiné of folklore literature has existed among the Croats from the seventeenth century onwards. About the middle of the eighteenth century it began to acquire the essential traits of a standard language *in statu nascendi*. This is a most fundamental turning point and the very beginning of the Neo-štokavic standardization among the Croats, even though the intellectual and artistic achievements of this cultural activity were quite modest and the young standard (language) did not embrace the whole Croatian area, but only its major part. . . .

"The roots of this process of standardization lie in the popular edificational literature of the seventeenth century, and this literature, in its turn, has a base in the whole of the older Croatian writing, mediaeval and renaissance. The Neo-štokavic Croatian standard as it exists today is thus an integral part of the whole of Croatian literary language, and is heir to the whole of its potential expression and its stylistic values."[36]

From the Renaissance up to the 19th century, the term 'Illyrian' was often used to designate the Croatian language or a native of Croatia. Since the Croats settled in the Roman Province of Illyricum during the seventh century, a popular belief prevailed that the Croats were descendants of the Illyrians and so were often referred to by this term.

After the French victory of 1809 at Wagram, Austria was compelled to cede its South Slavs lands to France. Napoleon grouped these lands to form a new political entity, the Illyrian Provinces, which were incorporated into the French Empire. This Napoleonic creation lasted only four years, but it gave new impetus to the Croat search for a national identity. It was in the Illyrian Provinces (1809-1814) that there developed a sense of Slav unity and national awareness which manifested itself in the Illyrian movement of the 1830s which stressed the need for cooperation among Slavs and sought the unification of all South Slavs in the Habsbourg monarchy. The movement was led by the liberal nobility and the intelligentsia that was associated with it.

The Nineteenth Century

Early in the nineteenth century, in 1814 the Serb Vuk Stefanović Karadžić (1787—1864) published a small grammar *Pismenica* (in *što-je*). In the meantime, he compiled in collaboration with the Slovenian scholar Jernej Kopitar (1780—1844) an excellent trilingual dictionary of 36,000 entries in *što-je* (*Srpski rječnik, Lexicon Serbico-Germanico-Latinum*) which came out in 1818 and was to be reedited in 1852, 1898, 1935 and 1966. Kopitar provided the Latin and German equivalents to Serbian terms in this dictionary.

This event was of great consequence for the Serbs who up to then had written either in a Russianised Church-Slavonic or in *"Slaveno-Serbski"*.[37] These artificial hybrid languages were genetically related but had different uses and hampered the development of the local vernacular for literary purposes. Karadžić rebelled against traditional Church Slavonic and his book *Description of the Serbian Language According to the Speech of the Common Man*, published in 1814/15, helped the literature of the popular language to a breakthrough. Vuk's mentor in Vienna, Kopitar, had also urged Vuk to take up the study of Serbian and Croatian folk songs, folk tales and gnomic expressions.

However, circumstances were quite different for the Croats.[38] At the time of the Illyrian movement (1830s) inspired by Ljudevit Gaj and his associates and under the influence of Romanticism which introduced the cult of nationalism, and the intellectual and political revival, they proclaimed that the literary language of the Ragusans and the other *što* writers was the literary koiné which would lead the Croat people to linguistic and national unity. The name "Illyrian" is reminiscent of Napoleonic Illyria and during the national awakening, which occurred in post-Napoleonic Central and Eastern Europe, political emancipation was accompanied by language

31

revivals, with emphasis laid on folk traditions.

Under this momentum the old literary language of Dubrovnik was an influence of primary importance in the creation of the new Croatian literary language. This literary koiné or national language played a part in unification and became the symbol of supralocal, ethnic and cultural identification. It was used from the outset in 1836 in scholarship and journalism as well as in poetry and literary prose. "Moreover, it should not be forgotten that the chief model for the reformers was the language of the almost exclusively poetical renaissance literature of Dubrovnik. While the accepted Croatian literary language eventually diverged from this model in a number of respects its influence was paramount: without its existence Croatian might have developed in quite different directions".[39]

Thus apart from stimulating intense creativity in literature, this new literary language became the vehicle and symbol of the Croatian national movement.

In Zagreb, where he settled, helped by Count Janko Drašković, Gaj in January 1835 began to publish his daily paper, the *Novine Horvatske* (Croatian News) with a weekly literary supplement the *Danica* (Morning Star). At the beginning of 1836 he changed his paper's name to *Ilirske Narodne Novine* (Illyrian National Gazette) and started preaching the doctrine of "Illyrianism", in other words the union of the South Slavs. Gaj formulated the immediate tasks of the Illyrian movement — the struggle for the development of the Croatian national culture and language, which the ideologists of the movement attempted to represent as common to all Southern Slavs. However, he failed to convince all his fellow Slavs. The Serbs rejected "Illyrianism" with its Western connotations almost unanimously and Karadžić himself, as a Serbian patriot, did not want the formation of a single nation. The 'South Slavs' idea was an intellectual concept, an act of faith, not the outcome of historical development. Slovenes, Croats and Serbs were separated by their past and by their political allegiance and were also sharply divided by religion and by culture.

In 1842 the Austrian authorities in Vienna forbade the use

of the word "Illyrian" and Gaj had to change the name of his paper back to "Croat". "Babukić, as the effective editor of Gaj's journal *Danica Ilirska*, for some years exercised considerable authority in directing the course of the new literary Croatian. Apart from his native štokavic speech habits he was profoundly influenced by the old literary language of Dubrovnik. This influence became very apparent in the language of the articles in *Danica* and gave rise to a number of protests. The language of Dubrovnik, moreover, strongly affected the two foremost poets of the Illyrian movement, Ivan Mažuranić and Stanko Vraz".[40] In 1844 Ivan Mažuranić supplied the two missing cantos (XIV and XV) for an edition of a huge epic poem, *Osman*, composed by the renowned poet from Dubrovnik Ivan Gundulić (1589—1638), and in 1846 published his own epic poem *Smrt Smail-age Čengića* (The Death of Smail-Aga) which was certainly influenced by Gundulić's *Osman*.

We are confronted here with a phenomenon that occurs relatively often in the history of languages: a classical work (*Osman*) standing at the beginning of literary development which leads to the imitation and emulation of its language.

In *Foundations of the Slavonic Grammar of the Illyrian Dialect* (1836) Vjekoslav Babukić established standards for the national literary language that were subsequently adopted by writers, scholars and the press. Printing presses, reading rooms, and in 1845, the subdepartment of Croatian language and literature at the Zagreb Academy were established. In 1848, Croatian was recognized as the official language in Croatia and Slavonia.

The "Illyrians" attempted to unify all the *što* subdialects into a single literary language and they followed with great interest the parallel efforts of Vuk Karadžić among the Serbs. But while, in his reform of the literary language, Vuk completely and deliberately broke away from the "Slaveno-Serbski" tradition and from the past, the Croats conversely sought to unify the regional literary languages on the foundation of tradition.[41] The result of action by Vuk and the "Illyrian" Croats was that the Serbs (especially those who

33

lived in Austria-Hungary) and the Croats decided to choose the *što-ije* dialect as a common literary language. The differences which appeared from the outset of this attempt, most of which survive today, may be attributed to the influence of different traditions of the communities concerned.

The culminating point of all these efforts to create a written language common to all Croats and all Serbs was the "Vienna Literary Agreement" (*Bečki književni dogovor*") of 1850. It was signed by the Croatian writers Ivan Mažuranić, Dimitrije Demeter, Ivan Kukuljević, Vinko Pacel and Stjepan Pejaković, by the Serbian philologists Djuro Daničić and Vuk S. Karadžić and the Slovenian linguist Franz Milkošič. It is worth noting that the most outstanding Croat linguists of the period, Vjekoslav Babukić, Antun Mažuranić, Bogoslav Šulek and Ljudevit Gaj, did not attend the Vienna meeting and in 1862 one of the signatories, Ivan Mažuranić, rejected the stipulations of the "Vienna Literary Agreement". Even the other signatories (Demeter, Pacel) did not observe the Vienna Agreement for different reasons. The spokesman of Croatian national revival in Dalmatia, Ante Kuzmanić (1807-1879), the editor of Zadar periodicals *Zora dalmatinska* (1844) and *Glasnik dalmatinski* (1849-1855), together with his collaborators, Ṡ. Starčević, M. Šantić, S. Ivićević, defended the *što-i* dialect and strognly opposed the Vienna Agreement. The first article of this Agreement says that "it is unreasonable to mix dialects to create a new language unknown to the people, but it is better to choose one of the existing dialects as the written language". The second article recommends the choice of an *i-je* dialect, that of East-Herzegovina, writing the two syllables *-ije-* (*bijelo*) and the one syllable *-je-* (*bjelina*), *-e-* (*mreža*), *-i-* (*donio*), as the written language for the Serbs and Croats. This choice was dictated by the widespread domination of the *i-je* language, the celebrated *i-je* literature of Dubrovnik and the *i-je* folk poetry.

At that time it might have been thought that the way was open for a common Serbo-Croat written language. But in the nineteenth century the Serbs and the Croats were split among three, and even four, States, some in the Principality (later the Kingdom) of Serbia, some in the Dual Monarchy of Austria-Hungary (Croatia—Slavonia—Dalmatia—Istria and Vojvodina) and others in the Ottoman Empire (Bosnia and Herzegovina), while the Montenegrins had a principality of their own. A uniform cultural policy was therefore not feasible as throughout the 19th century there was surprisingly little real contact between the Serbs and the Croats.[42] Futhermore, national feeling and the spirit of independence grew steadily stronger in Croatia as well as in Serbia. All this played a great part in the question of the common language. It must also be said that in their respective attempts to reform the language Gaj and Karadžić were not pursuing the same end.[43] Vuk's reform was specifically Serbian and the Croats criticised his Serb particularism.

The representatives of the Illyrian movement mainly sought to unify the written language with a common orthography, despite variations in pronunciation. Thus they introduced and wrote the letter ě which stood for /ije/, /je/, /i/ or /e/ and was pronounced accordingly in different štokavic dialects. They regarded the language and grammar of Karadžić as provincial because it took account of one single dialect exclusively, the Herzegovina neo-što, and disregarded the ča and kaj dialects, while the Illyrian grammarians (Vjekoslav Babukić (1812—1875) and Antun Mažuranić (1805—1888)) also took account, in their grammars, of old forms and words in other dialects such as kaj and ča, and even in the Slovene language. They sought to achieve linguistic and national unity by a gradual fusion of što sub-dialects in a common language. They did not create a new Croatian standard but merely extended the existing štokavic standard to čakavic and kajkavic regions; and if the Croat language reveals a particular physiognomy inside the South Slavic family it is due to the čakavic and kajkavic substratum and to the South-Western form of štokavic (superstratum). "Thus the Illyrian movement itself appears to be the beginning of one period in the growth of the Neo-Štokavian Croatian standard and the end of a preceding one. This is clearly illustrated by the fact that the Illyrian grammarians only continued the work of their Pre-Illyrian predecessors".[44]

Actually, in the formation of the national language and in the development of the Croatian koiné based on the *što* dialect, borrowings from the *ča* and *kaj* dialects have played a great part. It is often forgotten how much of the Croatian vocabulary is produced by intimate borrowing from its dialects. The *ča* dialect contributed maritime and nautical terms. Furthermore *ča* was the channel for most of the Mediterranean terms and, for a long time, of Italian borrowings, while *kaj* supplied many words of Germanic origin and *što* provided Turkish borrowings such as *čamac, čarapa, ćelav, čizma, deva, div, dućan, duhan, džep, jastuk, kalup, kat, sanduk, šećer, tava, top, torba,* etc.

A number of gnomic expresions have come into literary Croat from one or other of its dialects through literature in which influential authors (Šenoa, Kovačić, etc.) deliberately chose to use dialectal words and phrases. Some of these have proved to be vivid and expressive and so have become permanent and have even reached the spoken language, e.g. *ni uha ni sluha, trbuhom za kruhom,* etc.

The Illyrian movement set itself the objective of creating a language common to all South Slavs, from Villach (Beljak) in Austria to Varna in Bulgaria, adopting thus Humboldt's view that: *»Die wahre Heimat ist eigentlich die Sprache«*. Its programme was eclectic from the linguistic point of view, tolerating the admixture of dialects, but essentially based on the *što* dialect. However, the Serbs were loath to adopt the Latin alphabet, which the Serbian priests denounced as a devilish machination of Rome's to seduce them from the true, Orthodox, faith while the Slovenes were unwilling even reluctant to abandon their own vernacular. That is why Ljudevit Gaj, the real founder of the Illyrian movement and the reformer of Croatian spelling and orthography, did not sign the Vienna Agreement of 1850 which was to legislate on the written language of the Serbs and Croats. In the end, this Agreement amounted to no more than a manifesto since it was not observed by either the Croatian or the Serbian press and writers.

Furthermore, the "Illyrians", not only sought the unification of the language but also felt the need to introduce a great
many new words for the use of secondary schools and
universities, science and technology. These were, unfortunately, missing from the dictionary of Karadžić, who drew
upon popular speech and village folklore. Since a vocabulary,
if it is to fulfil its purpose, must be constantly expanding and
unceasingly renewed, the "Illyrians" regarded linguistic
borrowing as a normal process of lexical enrichment because
it increases the powers of expression of an idiom which tends
to become the standard language of a nation. Their deliberate
selection of lexical borrowings to enrich the written language
corresponded to their desire to create a uniform language for
the use of all Southern Slavs.

Two special forms of word-borrowing should be briefly
mentioned. The first, loan-translation or 'calque' is exemplified
by *zemljopis*, after the Czech *zemépis*, which was formed
on the pattern *geografija*.

Internal borrowing is more important: this occurs when
one dialect of a language adopts words from another. Such
borrowings are called 'internal loans'. Actually, *kaj* words
are found in the texts of the grammarian Babukić and his con-
temporaries. At the same time a great many borrowings
are found from other Slav languages, especially Czech and
Russian.[45] It should be noted that it was upon the idea of the
reciprocal enrichment of the various Slavic languages that
the Slovak poet Ján Kollár, the author of *The Daughter of
Sláva* (*Slávy dcera*, 1824), based his theory of literary reciprocity, a manifesto of intellectual Panslavism. In his
influential treatise *O Litérarnéj vzájemnosti mezi kmeny a
nářečimi slavskými*, published also in Gaj's *Danica* in 1836,
Kollár advocated literary cooperation among the Slavonic
peoples. It should also be noted that in his *Brief Basis for a
Croatian-Slavonic Orthography*, written in 1830, Gaj advocated
reform of the Croatian alphabet on the lines of the Czech
transcription. However, Panslavism evoked no response from
the Slav Congress which met in Prague on 2 June 1848; "Pan-
Slavism had sense only as a translation into racial mysticism

37

of the Byzantine and Orthodox heritage shared by some Slav peoples, and almost all those present at Prague were Western and Roman Catholic'' (A.J.P. Taylor, *Europe: Grandeur and Decline*, London, 1967, p. 39).

The rise of the Slavic written languages and literaratures in the first half of the nineteenth century had been characterized by the ideas, if not of Panslavism, at any rate of "Slavic mutuality", that is of a broad give-and-take among Slavic languages and literatures and of Austroslavism, i.e. the idea of maintaining Slav solidarity and a modest national existence in the Habsburg monarchy. Less than a century later, in 1937, the Czech philologist, M. Weingart, found that the old reciprocity of the romantic period had been replaced by "an evident distaste for the influence of another Slavic literary language, particularly a neighbouring one. . . There is in this a visible turning away from the ideas of romanticism and the direct opposite of what was then demanded by Jan Kollár".[46]

Regarding vocabulary-expansion, three main methods were advocated by the Illyrians: (1) the adoption of dialect-words into the standard language and the revival of obsolete words; (2) the borrowing of words from other Slavic languages, especially Czech and loan-translations from German; (3) the coining of words from native elements by affixation and compounding.

In the German-Illyrian dictionary of Ivan Mažuranić and Jakov Užarević of 1842 (*Njemačko-ilirski slovar*) a great many Bohemianisms and some Russianisms are already to be found (e.g. *časopis, čitanka, lučba, narječje, obred, obzor, opseg, okolnost, povod, pokus, točan, točka, vodovod* etc.).[47] Bogoslav Šulek (1816—1895), the founder of Croatian scientific terminology and modern lexicography, proceeded in the same way in his three dictionaries. The first, entitled *Njemačko-Hrvatski Rječnik* (German-Croatian Dictionary) of 1860, played a great part in fixing linguistic norms of standard language. The second, entitled *Hrvatsko-Njemačko-Talijanski Rječnik Znanstvenog Nazivlja* (Croatian-German-Italian Dictionary of Scientific Terminology) of 1874 and edited by Šulek, was in reality the joint work of the Zagreb philologists, namely

Vatroslav Jagić, Josip Torbar, Bogoslav Šulek, Franjo Erjavec, etc.[48] This work was supplemented by the Dictionary of German-Croatian Technological Terminology (*Rječnik Njemačko-Hrvatskoga Tehnologičkoga Nazivlja*), compiled and edited in Zagreb in 1881 by the Club of Engineers and Architects. A few years earlier, in 1868, Ivan Dežman's Dictionary of Medical Terminology (*Rječnik Liječničkog Nazivlja*) was published and in 1879 Šulek's Yugoslav Botanical Nomenclature (*Jugoslavenski Imenik Bilja*).

Dežman's older colleague, Ante Schwartz (1832—1880), contributed considerably to the creation of Croatian medical terminology. His work "Descriptive Anatomy. . ." (*Opisna anatomija ili razudbarstvo čovječjega tiela*), 2 vols., Zagreb, 1873—1874, was designed as a manual for Croatian students and is the first major medical work in Croatian. He was also the founder and the first editor of the "Medical Journal" (*Liečnički Viestnik*) (1877—1880). Together Schwartz and Dežman elaborated the plan for further collection and creation of Croatian medical terminology.[49]

In addition, two Croatian grammars came out at that time: A. Mažuranić's *Slovnica hrvatska*, 1859, and V. Jagić's *Gramatika jezika hrvatskoga*, 1864.

Thus the necessary conditions for the development of the literary and learned language were all satisfied at the time of the foundation of the Yugoslav Academy in 1866 and of the University of Zagreb in 1874. These two institutions stimulated a Croatian cultural revival which looked for inspiration to Prague, Vienna and the West. The lexicographer Šulek and his collaborators adopted words from the *kaj* dialect (*bedast, jâl, huškač, kazalište, krabulja, klobuk, kukac, kupelj, ličilac, ladanje, oponašati, pošast, preuzetan, preuzetnost, pospan, prenavljanje, priprost, proštenje, rastepsti, rublje, šalica, tjedan, tok, vrhnje, veža, zdenac, zakutan, zipka, zračiti, žohar*, etc.) as well as some from the *ča* dialect (*blanja, blanjati, klesar, klesati, kljova, konoba, jalan, spužva, škrinja, škver*, etc) and many other words which are common to both *kaj* and *ča* dialects (such as *brenta, pošast, haran, hlače, okno, hiniti, himba, nijetiti, piknja, črknja, obijest, korjenika, rubac, poprijeko, košarica, prhak, srh,* etc.). They also introduced into the written language a number of cultural borrowings, Bohemianisms and Russianisms as well as neologisms, thereby enabling the popular language to meet the needs of both literature and science. The influence of Czech on Croat in the lexical sphere was considerable, not least because of the activities of the Slovak Šulek who settled in Zagreb, capital of Croatia, and played an important part in the language reform movement. His three dictionaries have been studied by Ljudevit Jonke who has shown Šulek's profound influence upon the Croatian language. Jonke has clearly shown the importance of Czech in Šulek's work and notably of P.J. Šafařik's *Německo-český slovník vědeckého názvosloví pro gymnasia a reálné školy.*[50]

The new terms and turns of phrase introduced by Šulek have made it possible to express all the ideas resulting from the progress of science and the transformations of social life as well as new high-level concepts. Šulek also revived many words from the older language, notably the words recorded by the seventeenth and eighteenth-century lexicographers, adapting existing old words to new uses. It is clear that in the sphere of vocabulary he wished to remain, as did the "Illyrians", as close as possible to the language of tradition. Šulek also replaced many words of Turkish or German origin, recorded by Karadžić in his Dictionary, by native ones, thus *bakar, cigla, ćuprija, kazan, odžak, pendžer,* etc. were replaced by *mjed, opeka, most, kotao, dimnjak, prozor,* etc. It was therefore inevitable that the "Illyrian" (or, later, Croatian) literary language should move further and further away from the language of Karadžić.

However, while Šulek's vocabulary was not to be accepted in full, its penetration into the written language was so deep that even today the importance of his contribution is still recognised; we need cite only a few words: *bjelokost, brzojav, caklina, dionica, dojam, draguljar, dražba, dušik, geslo, glazba, gmaz, kipar, kolotur, kolodvor, latica, naklada, njihalo, otopina, pelud, plin, ploha, poduzetnik, pokost, pokus, postotak, promjer, razina, sadra, skladište, smjer, stanovit, stroj,*

*sustav, tiskara, tlak, titraj, tvar, tvornica, srećka, tvrtka, za-
klada, zasada, znanost, žarište,* etc. That is why there are other
equivalents for such words in Serbian, namely, *slonovača,
telegram, gleđ, akcija, utisak, juvelir, licitacija, azot, parola,
muzika, gmizavac, vajar, čekrk, stanica, cvetni list, izdanje, klat-
no, rastvor, polen (cvetni prah), gas, ravan, preduzimač, firnajz,
opit, procenat, prečnik, nivo, gips, magacin, pravac, izvestan,
mašina, sistem, štamparija, pritisak, oscilacija, materija,
fabrika, loz, firma, zadužbina, princip, nauka, žiža,* etc. The
subsequent development of the Croatian literary language
has shown that it is impossible to do without a number of
words introduced by Šulek. Šulek is also largely responsible for the creation of Croat military terminology.
From 1870 onwards he translated from Hungarian (into Croat)
twenty booklets dealing with army life and military terminology. In 1953 the renowned linguist Petar Skok described
the lexicographer Šulek as a linguistic genius, noting especially
his skill in creating neologisms from resources within the
language.

The lexical enrichment and evolution of the Croatian
language in the nineteenth century took two directions; firstly,
the use of words and expressions taken from the *kaj* and *ča*
dialects and, secondly, the borrowing and adaptation (by
calque) of foreign words.[51] At the same time Croatian has
attained the unification which was one of the aims of the nineteenth century language reformers. In the second half of the
nineteenth century the linguistic formation of the literary
language was under the auspices of the so-called Zagreb
philologic school. Continuing the work of Gaj and the grammarians Vjekoslav Babukić and Antun Mažuranić, the school
acquired its greatest hearing under the direction of the
philologist Adolf Veber Tkalčević (1825—1892)[52] and the
lexicographer B. Šulek. Tkalčević's philological work and
grammars and Šulek's dictionaries codified the usage and
established the standards of the language of that period in
accordance with literary tradition. Veber's Croatian grammar
(*Slovnica hrvatska*, 1871) had several editions, 1873², 1876³
but was later replaced by M. Divković's Croatian grammar

41

(*Hrvatska Gramatika za srednje škole, I Oblici*, 1879, *II Sintaksa*, 1881) used as a textbook in secondary schools. It was during this period that the Croat language was consciously expanded in vocabulary and standardized in spelling and grammar so that it could increasingly function as the language of government and of advanced civilisation and technology. The legislative, constitutional terminology elaborated between 1853 and 1887, and the statute laws published during this period, strictly comply with the orthographic and grammatical norms of the Zagreb philological school. All the official, legislative enactments of that period were collected and published in book form by Milan Smrekar in *Ustavno zakonoslovlje* (1883).[53]

In 1866 the Serbian philologist Đuro Daničić (1825—1882) came to Zagreb as Secretary of the newly founded South Slav Academy of Fine Arts and Science. He immediately began work on the *Dictionary of the Croat or Serbian Language*, edited by the Academy from 1880 to 1976. The purpose of his cooperation with his Zagreb collaborators in the Academy was to avoid new and unnecessary differences between Croat and Serb and, if possible, to try to close the gaps between the two languages. In their common effort, they tried to develop a Croatian literary language that would be based on Neo-štokavic popular speech and (Neo-štokavic) folklore literature and to determine language elements to be standardized.[54]

During this period a linguistic rapprochement was promoted by some prominent Croatians as a good foundation for a cultural and possible political unification. In Bishop Strossmayer the Croats possessed the leading Slav statesman of the Dual Monarchy and the only one of European importance. He dreamed of a union of the South Slavs round Croatia and the South Slav Academy, which he had founded in 1866, gave cultural expression to this idea. Strossmayer's campaign for the unification of the Southern Slavs could not stand up against the Serbian dream of a "Greater Serbia" and against Habsburg centralization. On the other hand, Croatian ideas of Illyrian unity had lost much of their popularity with the rise of the Party of Croat state rights led by Ante Starčević (d. 1896). In 1861,

Ante Starčević helped found the Party of Rights which developed a radical programme of complete independence of Croatia and genuine patriotism called *pravaštvo* (rights). Starčević led his followers in a continuing struggle against the Austrian and Hungarian oppressors but eventually he tried to work with Vienna to set up Croatia as the third State in the Empire.[55]

Daničić was the most fervent partisan and supporter of Vuk Karadžić's views on language reform, which he set forth in the *Survey of the Dictionary (of the Academy)* (*Ogled Rječnika*) in 1878. The first volume, published in 1881, and subsequent volumes of this dictionary were elaborated strictly in accordance with Karadžić's programme, which was often contrary to the Croat literary tradition. Thus the lexical stock of the rich kajkavic literature, which had flourished in Northern Croatia since the sixteenth century, has been largely omitted from this 23 quarto volume Dictionary while its first volumes make scarcely any reference to modern Croat literature. Daničić even ignored Šulek's dictionaries in compiling the materials for the Dictionary of Academy although the subsequent editors Budmani, Maretić, etc. consulted Šulek's lexicographical work and referred to it more and more.[56] In this historical but not pan-dialectal comprehensive dictionary, the emphasis is laid more upon the origin and history of words than on their current usage. Such a dia-chronic overall strategy of the Dictionary of the Academy based on historical principles is alien to the purposes of synchronic description. This dictionary clearly bears the imprint of the belated Romantic movement, with its veneration for what was old, organic and of popular origin and its rejection of what was new, artificial and cultivated, which strongly encouraged its compilers to turn their attention to the past, to the folk poetry (songs), folk tales and proverbs. In Croatia, particularly, there was also a nostalgia for a 'great', 'heroic' past, sung in folk songs, to compensate for the national setbacks in the Austro-Hungarian empire. However, no Croat, during that period, looked outside the frontiers of the Monarchy for the solution to their national problem.

The Croats knew that political unification of Croatia and Serbia would inevitably mean Serbian domination and the thought was unbearable to them.

Following the same phonetic and linguistic principles as Vuk Karadžić, the principles of "write as you speak and read as it is written", and thus breaking with morphophonemic, "etymological" orthography and written Croat tradition, Ivan Broz published in Zagreb his manual of Orthography (1892), and Tomislav Maretić his Grammar (1899), based only on the writings of Vuk, Daničić and several writers who followed them. Finally, in 1901, there appeared Broz-Iveković's Dictionary of the Croat Language. Maretić's and Iveković's concepts in those works were severely criticized by Vatroslav Jagić who was a professor at Vienna University, and away from Zagreb. His criticism censured especially Iveković's work, who after Broz's death completed the compilation of the Dictionary. In this Dictionary 80 per cent of the (52 279) entries have been taken from štokavic folk poetry, folk tales and proverbs, while many čakavic and kajkavic terms (such as *darežljiv, darežljivost, krstitke, imetak, podroban, poplun, priuštiti, propuh, strop, tjedan*, etc.) used in contemporary Standard Croat, have been left out. Moreover, thousands of words of the 19th century štokavic literary Croat have not been entered in this dictionary. Neglecting the synchronic study of *kaj* and *ča* dialects and of contemporary literary language, the authors held, as did Herman Paul (1846—1921) in his *Principles of the History of Language,* that only a historical study of language had scholarly and scientific value. Broz, Iveković and Maretić are often referred to as Zagreb followers of Vuk Karadžić, yet they were also very much influenced by the Junggramatiker linguistic school of the late nineteenth century. They believed that the štokavic vernacular was the natural and primary language whereas the written language was secondary. Therefore they considered that the Standard language of the Croats was not the one which developed in Croat literature but štokavic vernacular, as used in oral folk poetry, tales and proverbs. They also hypostatized language as an independent organism, developing according

44

to equally hypostatized laws independently of the writers. Though they worked along the same lines as Vuk and Daničić, they were not blind followers of Vuk as is often rather simplistically stated. Thus Iveković, in the preface to his Dictionary (page V.) writes: "One can also see how much some of Vuk's partisans have exaggerated by maintaining that the words which are not to be found in his Dictionary are not valid; in our language (Croatian) there are thousands of valid and beautiful words which Vuk did not and could not know". Twenty years later, in the "Preliminary Part" (*Pristup*) of his *Language Counsellor* (*Jezični Savjetnik*) of 1924, Maretić writes: "Only people of obsolete principles and limited mind can refer today to Vuk, Daničić and Iveković". Maretić was also highly critical of Daničić's omission of kajkavic words from the Dictionary of the Zagreb Academy.[57] To make up for this deficiency the Historico-Philological Department of the Zagreb Academy decided in 1936 to edit a separate Dictionary of the kajkavic dialect. However the actual work on the compilation of this dictionary started only in 1973. The dictionary will consist of two quarto volumes and will contain all the terms of the literary kajkavic from the 16th century to the present day, about 100 000 units. Unfortunately the words of the contemporary kajkavic vernacular will not be included in this dictionary. Broz, Iveković and Maretić were also opposed to the binominal expression 'Serbo-Croatian' which was later in Yugoslavia imposed by Belgrade governments. Thus Broz, in his work *Croatian Literature*, considering the different names by which the Croatian language has been called through the centuries, concludes: "The natural language of a people should be called after the name of the respective peoples to which it refers; and since history knows only two national names for Croatians and Serbians, it follows that the language of the Croatian people must be called the Croatian language, and that of the Serbian people the Serbian language". (I. Broz, *Crtice iz hrvatske književnosti*. Vol. I. Hrvatska književnost, Zagreb, 1886, p. 160.)

Broz's Orthography (*Hrvatski pravopis*, 1892) and Maretić's Grammar (*Gramatika hrvatskog jezika*, 1899) were used as

45

textbooks in secondary schools in Croatia by the turn of the century. Maretić's school grammar dominated Croatian classrooms from 1899 to 1928 during which time it went through ten editions. ''The final standardization of written Croat at the end of the last century did not introduce a new standard language among the Croats, but only removed the last controversial points in the already existing usage which functioned in unbroken continuity. It can even be observed that among the solutions proposed by the Zagreb followers of Karadžić, only those which correspond to traits prevailing in the neo-štokavic dialects of the Croatian area were eventually accepted''.[58]

In short, all these facts, connected with the formation of the Croatian language in the nineteenth century, prove that the evolution of a language cannot be directed by virtue of an Agreement of a few literary men.

For that matter the Serbs were no more faithful to the terms of the Vienna Agreement of 1850 than the Croats. In the new Serbian literature of the nineteenth century the *neo-što-e* dialect far outdistanced the *neo-što(i)je* dialect. Although *i-je* was spoken in a few small regions of West Serbia, most Serbs used the *-e-* variant of Vojvodina, since the Serbian literary centre in the nineteenth century was the town of Novi Sad in Vojvodina. This town was also the seat of the *Matica srpska*, a literary society, founded in 1826, which became the cultural centre of all Serbian life of that day.

This *što-e* written dialect has developed differently from the *i-je* language. In the second half of the nineteenth century it was enriched by an independent learned and scientific terminology with a substantial Russian contribution[59], in exactly the same way as a new terminology was formed among the Croats under the influence of the Czech language. Furthermore, since the Principality of Serbia resisted the language reform of Vuk Karadžić up to 1868, the Serbian people, both in Hungary (Vojvodina) and in Serbia itself, using the *što-e* speech of Vojvodina and Šumadija in the neighbourhood of Belgrade, accepted Vuk's language as the standard literary language towards the end of the nineteenth century, but in the alternative form of *što-e*, thus creating a linguistic schism.

Vuk was aware that the Serbs regarded the *-ije* dialect as being Croatian. In the preface to his collection of folk poems, *Narodna Srbska pesmarica; čast vtora* (Vienna, 1815), in which are recorded Serbian poems in *-e* dialect and Croatian ones in *-ije* dialect, Vuk writes that he recorded the poems as he had heard them, i.e. in two different dialects, *-e* and *-ije*. He also writes: "If I had recorded all (the poems) in Herzegovinian dialect (e.g. *djevojka, djeca, vidjeti* etc.) then the people in Srem (especially townspeople) would have said: "but why is this man imposing on us the Croatian language?"". It was the Serbian writers of the intellectual centres of the North, Novi Sad and Belgrade, who imposed the *-e-* speech as the basis of literary Serbian. In this way they departed from Vuk's language, for it is the good writers who determine literary languages and not the grammarians. The grammarian is only needed afterwards. The Serbian literary language today represents a compromise between the language of Vuk and that of the literary centres of Novi Sad and Belgrade, between the reform of Vuk and the tradition of Dositej Obradović.[60]

"We can only speculate what might have happened had the Serbs accepted the Vienna Agreement completely, but no one can doubt that it is too late for that now. On the other hand, the Croatian standard did unify and does now unify all Croats into a single speech community. This criterion perhaps more clearly than any other one supports the autonomy of the Croatian standard".[61]

Apart from the external factors of political, social, economic and religious conditions which played an important part in the formation of Croat and Serbian literary languages, the margin of variations and the dissimilarities between the two languages are even greater when one takes into account the internal evolution of the two languages. The changes were taking place on the phonetic and semantic levels, the phonetic alteration always resulting in a displacement of relationship between the signifier (*significans*) and the signified (*significatum*). The outcome is that we have a common signifier for two different concepts in Serbian and Croatian. Let us examine by contrastive analysis some of the differences in this field between

47

the two languages, for instance:

brijač
- Sb. 'a razor' Cr. *britva*
- Cr. 'a barber' Sb. *berberin, brica*

čas
- Sb. 'an hour, lesson' Cr. *sat*
- Cr. 'a moment' (cf. Sb. *časovnik* 'a wristwatch, Cr. (*ručni*) *sât* or *ura*, Sb. *časovničar* 'watchmaker' Cr. *urar*)

čedan adj.
- Sb. 'innocent' Cr. *nevin*
- Cr. 'humble'

četvorka
- Sb. 'a playing card with four pips' Cr. *četvrtica*
- Cr. 'quadrille' (dance) Sb. *kadril*

dogled
- Sb. 'binocle' Cr. *dalekozor*
- Cr. 'purview, range of vision'

dvojiti
- Sb. 'to distinguish'
- Cr. 'to doubt, to call in question'

gotov adj.
- Sb. 'ready' Cr. *spreman*
- Cr. 'finished, done, complete'
  - cf. Sb. *gotovost* 'readiness' Cr. *pripravnost, spremnost*

ishlapio
- Sb. *izlapeo* 'senile' inf. *ishlapeti*
- Cr. 'evaporated' inf. *ishlapiti*

izvod
- Sb. 'an extract from the regulation' Cr. *izvadak*
- Cr. 'deduction = the process of drawing a conclusion'

kmet
- Sb. 'village headman'
- Cr. 'feudal serf, bondman'

kolovoz
- Sb. 'a track for wagons' Cr. *kolnik*
- Cr. 'August (month)'

kovčeg
- Sb. 'coffin' Cr. *lijes*
- Cr. 'suit-case' Sb. *kofer*

ličiti	Sb. 'to resemble' Cr. *sličiti, nalikovati* Cr. 'to paint' Sb. *molovati* (cf. Cr. *ličilac* 'house painter' Sb. *moler, farbar*
l(j)ekar	Sb. 'physician' Cr. *liječnik* Cr. 'chemist, pharmacist'
mapa	Sb. 'a geographical map' Cr. *zemljovid* Cr. 'a folder, an outer cover for papers'
mogućan	Sb. 'possible' Cr. *moguć* Cr. 'powerful, mighty'
naučnik	Sb. 'a scholar' Cr. *znanstvenik, učenjak* Cr. 'an apprentice' (cf. Sb. *nauka* 'science' Cr. *znanost*)
nepokretnost	Sb. 'immovables, real estate' Cr. *nekretnina* Cr. 'immovability, fixity'
obrt	Sb. 'a turn' Cr. *obrat* Cr. 'craftsmanship or trade'
odložiti	Sb. 'to postpone' Cr. *odgoditi* Cr. 'to take off, to lay away (aside)'
odojče	Sb. 'a suckling baby' Cr. *dojenče* Cr. 'a sucking-pig'
okolina	Sb. 'surroundings' Cr. *okolica,* (*okoliš*) Cr. 'milieu' Cf. Cr. *čovjekova okolina* 'environment' Sb. *čovekova* (*životna*) *sredina*
pomrčina	Sb. 'black-out' Cr. *zamračenje* Cr. 'eclipse' Sb. *pomračenje*
poručiti	Sb. 'to order' Cr. *naručiti* Cr. 'to send a message' (*poruka*—a message)
poslanik	Sb. 'M.P. Member of Parliament' Cr. *zastupnik* Cr. 'ambassador'

povr(ij)editi	Sb. 'to injure' Cr. *ozlijediti* Cr. 'to do wrong or injustice to'
poziv	Sb. 'vocation, a particular occupation or profession Cr. *zvanje* Cr. 'a calling or summons'
pravdati se	Sb. 'to justify oneself' Cr. *opravdavati se* Cr. 'to quarrel, to argue'
praznik	Sb. 'a holy day' (dies festus) Cr. *blagdan,* *svetkovina* Cr. 'any day of exemption from labour' Sb. *raspust*
pûk	Sb. 'regiment' (from Russian) Cr. *pukovnija* Cr. 'folk, people in general' (cf. *pučanstvo* population)
raspuštenica	Sb. 'a divorcee' Cr *rastavljena žena* Cr. 'a loose woman'
saobraćaj	Sb. 'street-traffic' Cr. *promet* Cr. 'intercourse, communication between individuals' (Sb. *saobraćajac* 'traffic policeman' Cr. *prometnik*; Sb. *saobraćajnica* Cr. *prometnica*)
saznati	Sb. 'to comprehend, to perceive' Cr. *spoznati* Cr. 'to learn, to come to know' (cf. Sb. *saznanje* Cr. *spoznaja*)
slovenski adj.	Sb. 'slavic' Cr. *slavenski* Cr. 'Slovene' Sb. *slovenački*
sočivo	Sb. 'lens' Cr. *leća* Cr. 'lentil' Sb. *leća*
sravniti	Sb. 'to compare' (from Russian) Cr. *usporediti* Cr. 'to flatten, to level'
stanica	Sb. 'a railway station' Cr. *kolodvor* Cr. 'a cell' (biol.) Sb. *ćelija*
stečaj	Sb. 'competition' Cr. *natječaj* Cr. 'bankruptcy'

stroj	Sb. 'a military file' (from Russian) Cr. *red* Cr. 'a machine' (from Czech) (Cr. *strojar*, Sb. *mašinista*)
sv(j)edočanstvo	Sb. 'school diploma (certificate)' Cr. *svjedodžba* Cr. 'testimony, evidence'
tečan	Sb. 'fluid, liquid' Cr. *tekući* Cr. 'tasteful, savoury' Sb. *ukusan*
tečnost	Sb. 'liquid' Cr. *tekućina* Cr. 'tastefulness' (cf. Cr. *tek* in *dobar tek* 'good appetite' Sb. *prijatno*)
tuča	Sb. 'fight' Cr. *tučnjava* Cr. 'hail = pellets of ice falling from the clouds'
udes	Sb. 'a traffic accident' Cr. *prometna nesreća* (cf. Sb. *desiti se* 'to happen' Cr. *dogoditi se* Cr. 'fate, destiny' (cf. D.Brozović, *Poruka o* *Udesu Riječi*, Jezik (1961/62 No.3 p.65-71))
ugao	Sb. 'angle' (geom.) Cr. *kut* Cr. 'corner' Sb. *ćošak*
ugljenik	Sb. 'carbon' Cr. *ugljik* Cr. 'coal-mine, colliery'
uzrast	Sb. 'age' Cr. *dob života* Cr. 'height (rate of growth)' *rast*
variti	Sb. 'to digest' Cr. *probavljati* Cr. 'to cook, to brew' (cf. Sb. *pivara* 'beer brew- ery' Cr. *pivovara* (from Czech); Cr. *varivo* 'boiled vegetables')
vjeđa	Sb. *veđa* 'eye-brow' Cr. 'eye-lid'
značaj	Sb. 'importance' Cr. *važnost* Cr. 'character'
zrak	Sb. 'a (sun) ray' Cr. *zraka* Cr. 'air' Sb. *vazduh*

These internal changes, which take place within the system of the language, are partly due to external influence such as borrowings from a neighbouring dialect (*ličiti* from *kaj*) or a neighbouring language (e.g. *sât* from Turkish, *ura* from Romance, *mapa* from German (*Mappe*), *stroj* and *zemljovid* from Czech, *kolodvor* borrowed from Slovene and modelled on the German *Bahnhof*).

Some other words that at first glance seem to be completely synonymous in Serbian and Croatian actually overlap in their meanings, which do not fully coincide. Thus the referential meaning and range of one word in Serbian might encompass the meanings of two words in Croatian. For example:

Sb. *bokser*	Cr. *boksač* 'a pugilist' Cr. *bokser* 'a brown dog', 'a knuckle-duster'
Sb. *crtati*	Cr. *crtati* 'to draw with a ruler' Cr. *risati* 'free hand drawing' (cf. *obris* 'outline')
Sb. *cepati*	Cr. *cijepati* 'to cut with an axe' Cr. *derati* 'to tear, to lacerate' (paper, clothes . . .)
Sb. *gnjurac*	Cr. *gnjurac* 'a bird' Cr. *ronilac* 'a diver, one who dives' (a man)
Sb. *igra*	Cr. *igra* 'a game' Cr. *ples* 'dance'
Sb. *jezuita*	Cr. *jezuit* 'a crafty, intriguing person' Cr. *isusovac* 'a member of Society of Jesus'
Sb. *lice*	Cr. *lice* 'a face' Cr. *osoba* 'a person'
Sb. *nedelja*	Cr. *nedjelja* 'Sunday' Cr. *tjedan* 'a week'
Sb. *osvetiti*	Cr. *osvetiti* 'to avenge' Cr. *posvetiti* 'to consecrate'
Sb. *porodica*	Cr. *porodica* 'blood related family' (derived from *rod* 'lineage') Cr. *obitelj* 'the nuclear family living under the same roof'

Sb. *povreda*	Cr. *povreda* 'offence, violation' Cr. *ozljeda* 'injury'
Sb. *pretstava*	Cr. *predstava* 'performance, show' Sb. *predodžba* (psych.) 'apperception'
Sb. *prost*	Cr. *prost* 'vulgar' Cr. *jednostavan* 'simple'
Sb. *rđav*	Cr. *hrđav* 'rusty' Cr. *zao* 'wicked, bad'
Sb. *sipati*	Cr. *sipati* 'to shoot grain (sand, gravel, rubble, earth) into something Cr. *točiti* (*lijevati*) 'to pour out the liquid, to pour away' (cf. also *nasuti* and *naliti*)
Sb. *spasti*	Cr. *spasti* 'to fall (drop) down' Cr. *spasiti* 'to save, rescue'
Sb. *sprovesti*	Cr. *sprovoditi* 'to escort (a prisoner)' Cr. *provoditi* 'to carry out'
Sb. *sveska* (f.)	Cr. *svezak* (m.) 'volume' Cr. *teka* (*bilježnica*) 'exercise book'
Sb. *topiti*	Cr. *topiti* 'to melt' Cr. *taliti* 'to smelt'
Sb. *ukus*	Cr. *ukus* 'taste' Cr. *okus* 'sense of taste'
Sb. *vetriti*	Cr. *hlapiti* 'to evaporize, to exhale' Cr. *vjetriti* 'to air'
Sb. *voz*	Cr. *vlak* 'train' Cr. *voz* 'waggon (of hay)' etc.

Finally it must be said that in *-e-* Serbian there are a great many homonyms due to the reflex of the paleo-Slavonic *jat*. To avoid confusion between homonyms, the *-e-* language has resorted to the creation of new terms, different from those used by the Croats. Thus the verb *potecati* (Cr. *potjecati*) 'to result from, to arise or come from', has been replaced in Serbian by the verb *poticati* to avoid a homonymic clash with the paradigmatic present forms *potečem, potečeš, poteče* etc. of the verb *poteći* 'to begin to flow'. But the latter form came into conflict with the verb *poticati* 'to incite, stimulate, encourage', which generated and entailed the creation of a new form *podsticati*; consequently we have:

Serbian *podsticati* (*podstrekavati*)   Croatian *poticati*
    ''   *poticati*   ''   *potjecati*[62].

Likewise the verb *natecati se* (Cr. *natjecati*) 'to compete, to contend', the paradigmatic forms of which enter into homonymic clash with the forms of the verb *nateći* 'to swell' i.e. *natečem, natečeš, nateče* etc., has been replaced in Serbian by the newly created infinitive *takmičiti se* or a loan word *konkurisati*; consequently we have in Serbian *takmičiti se, konkurisati*, in Croatian *natjecati se* (cf. also in Croat *natječaj* in Serbian *konkurs*).

To avoid confusion between the infinitive *povesti* 'to lead, to conduct' and the genitive singular *povesti* of the noun *povest* (Cr. *povijest*) 'history' the Serbs use the word *istorija* 'history' instead of *povest* which has become obsolete. In Croatian, on the contrary the word *povijest* is very much used just as the derivatives *povijestan, povjesničar, povjesnica, povjestica* 'legend' (cf. *Povjestice* by A. Šenoa).

To avoid homonymic clash between *on navesti* 'he announces' (Cr. *navijesti*) from *navestiti* (Cr. *navijestiti*) 'to announce' and the infinitive *navesti* (Cr. *navesti*) 'to induce, to bring about' a new infinitive *nagovestiti* has been created in Serbian to replace *navestiti*. Likewise, in *-e-* language there are no words *deva* 'camel', *mjed* 'brass', *odjel* 'department', *uvjet* 'condition' which would clash with the forms *déva* 'lass', *mêd* 'honey' or the oblique cases *u odélu* 'in a suit', *uveta* (gen. sing. of *uvo* 'ear'). The Serbian uses instead the borrowings *kamila, mesing, odelenje, uslov*, etc. All these phenomena of internal evolution, which are considerable, contributed to the lexical divergences between the two languages. Thus the Serbian adjectives *beo* 'white' and *smeo* 'daring' would normally correspond to the Croatian forms *bio* and *smio* but to avoid a homonymic clash with the past participles *bio* 'been' from *biti* 'to be' and *smio* 'allowed' from *smjeti* 'to be allowed', the Croats use the adjectives *bijel* 'white' and *smion* 'daring' instead.

In the same way, we find in Croatian "hyper-*i-je*-isms", that is to say, words whose root includes a -*je*- or an -*ije*- which are not due to the reflex of the palaeo-Slavonic *jat* (*ĕ*) but to the secondary lengthening of the vowel -*e*- (e.g. *istovetan* > *istovjetan*, *ozlediti* > *ozlijediti*, *ogrev* > *ogrjev*) or to paronymic attraction. This is particularly true of foreign loanwords whose root includes an -*e*- which popular etymology has sought to connect with indigenous roots which originally included a *jat* (cf. *vjeresija* 'credit' from Turkish *veresi*).[63] In this way divergences have accumulated, for the two variants -*e*- and -*ije*- have generated their own distinct linguistic innovations.

One could also mention the phonological oppositions which express semantic differences, particular to -(*i*)*je*- speech and unknown to -*e*- speech, for instance the opposition

/-ē-/ : /-jē-/

déva 'camel' : *djéva* 'lass'

/-ē-/ : /-jĕ-/

mêsnı (adj.) 'meaty' : *mjèsni* (adj.) 'local
svéže 'he ties' : *svjèže* (adj. n.) 'fresh'
mêd 'honey' : *mjȅd* 'brass';

/-ĕ-/ : /-jĕ-/

sèlo 'village' : *sjȅlo* 'sat' (past participle neuter of
  sjesti 'to sit down'
leti 'he flies' : *ljeti* 'in summer'

/-ĕ-/ : /-ije-/

bȅg 'Turkish bey' : *bȉjeg* 'flight, escape'
svèsti 'to reduce' : *svijesti* gen. sg. 'of the conscience'
izvèsti 'to lead out, guide' : *izvijesti* 'he informs'

/-ē-/ : */-ije-/*

svêt 'saint, holy' : *svîjet* 'people, world, universe'
nêma 'he has not' : *nijèma* (f.sg.) 'dumb'
plês 'dance : *plijes* 'mould'

/-jě-/ : */-ije-/*

sjèdīm 'I am sitting' : *sijèdim* 'My hair begins to turn grey'
djèla 'works' : *dijèla* (gen.sg.) 'of the part'

/-e-/ : */-je-/* : */-ije-/*

sèlo 'village' : *sjèlo* past participle of *sjesti* 'to sit down'
  : *sijèlo* 'evening reunion'

Consequently, literary Croat uses the phonetic oppositions *ije : i, je : i* to express semantic differences such as

nalijevati (from *lijevati*)	: *nalivati* (from *liti*)
prolijevati	: *prolivati*
slijevati	: *slivati*
ulijevati	: *ulivati*
zalijevati	: *zalivati*
naljev	: *naliv*
proljev	: *proliv*
slijev	: *sliv*
uljev	: *uliv*
zaljev	: *zaliv*
or	
dotjecati (from *teći*)	: *doticati* (from *ticati/taknuti*)
istjecati	: *isticati*
natjecati	: *naticati*
optjecati	: *opticati*
potjecati	: *poticati*
pretjecati	: *preticati*
pritjecati	: *priticati*
osijedjeti	: *osijediti* Sb. only *osedeti*
ostarjeti	: *ostariti* Sb. only *ostariti*
omršavjeti	: *omršaviti* Sb. only *omršaviti*
stjecati	: *sticati*
utjecati	: *uticati*
zatjecati	: *zaticati*

56

Some verbs issued from the same stem maintain semantic differences through this phonemic opposition *-jeti-* : *-iti-*

intransitive	transitive
bijeljeti 'to become white'	: *bijeliti* 'to whiten'
crnjeti 'to become black'	: *crniti* 'to blacken'
gŕdjeti 'to become ugly'	: *gŕditi* 'to scold'
grubjeti 'to become rough'	: *grúbiti* 'to roughen'
omiljeti 'to become dear'	: *omiliti* 'to endear'
opústjeti 'to become desert'	: *opústiti* 'to make desert'
oslijepjeti 'to become blind'	: *oslijepiti* 'to blind'
ožívjeti 'to become alive'	: *ožíviti* 'to put life into, to enliven', etc.

/ -i- / : / -je- /

gorila 'gorilla' : *gorjela* 'burnt' fem. past part. of *gorjeti* 'to burn'

/ -ĭ- / : / -ije- /

sȉr 'cheese' : *sȉjer* 'grey'

/ -ī- / : / -ije- /

vínca : *vijènca*, etc.

/ -ȋ- / : / -je- / : / -ije- /

sîna : *sjȅna* : *sȉjena*

/ -o- / : / -e- / : / -ije- /

tok : *tek* : *tijek*, etc.

A student with a superficial knowledge of 'Serbo-Croat' is very often unaware of these phonological oppositions which exist in literary Croat.[64] In addition, the prosodic-contour and stress-pattern, not to mention such paralinguistic features as rhythm and tempo so relevant in poetry, often differ in two languages (cf. Cr. *čìtāmo* — Sb. *čitámo*; Cr. *rȁdovi* — Sb. *rádovi*, etc). It follows from what has been said so far that "since every language has its distinctive peculiarities, the innate formal limitations — and possibilities — of one literature are never quite the same as those of another. The literature fashioned out of the form and substance of a language has the color and the texture of its matrix." (E. Sapir, *Language*, New York, 1939, p. 237). In brief, it is the literature that is carrying the language forward.

The above facts illustrate the difficulties to which one is exposed once one tries to guide the evolution of a language. The best intentions, the soundest theoretical justifications, are liable to clash with the living reality which often eludes the grasp of the reformer.

Does this mean that the Vienna Agreement was quite valueless? It is true that the development of the written language among the Croats and Serbs in the nineteenth century was somewhat uneven and the results were not quite those desired by Gaj or prophesied by Karadžić. Their work, however, was not wasted since the Croats as well as the Serbians have adopted the *što* dialect as the basis of their written literary language, although with two sharply different alphabets, traditions, literatures and loyalties. The differences which have developed with time are explained by two facts: the existence, firstly, of two distinct cultural centres, the cities of Zagreb and Belgrade, and, secondly, of two nations, the Croatian and the Serbian, who each regard their literary language as an essential national characteristic and a symbol of identity and national allegiance. The process by which national consciousness was slowly formed in Croatia and Serbia, though at first confined to elites of language-forming intelligentsias and myth-creating historians, was gradually extended to a much larger population and is an essential part of the history of nationalism. What is sometimes quite simply called the "genius" of a people is often contained in its national language and Ferdinand de Saussure says that "It is largely the language which makes the nation". Underlying this "national genius" there are always historical facts and social circumstances, and the nation itself is always a consequence of history, with ill-defined outlines. Language is, indeed, one of the most important objective components of the ethnic group and as a tributary of psychological data it plays its role in the formation of national character.[65] For that matter, there are undeniably subtle correlations between language, literature and other components of national cultures.

Consequently, at the outset of the twentieth century, even before the dismemberment of Austria-Hungary, the Croats and the Serbs used two standard literary languages, -e- among the Serbs and -ije- among the Croats, with a differentiated lexicon and dissimilarities in morphology and syntax; it is this divergence which persists today.[66] It is particularly striking in the lexicon. Actually, the differences apply primarily to the normative and standardized literary languages that can be consciously controlled by a cultural centre. To the difference of idioms is added the difference of scripts: the Cyrillic is that of the Orthodox Serbs; the Latin script is that of the Catholic Croats and of the Moslems of Bosnia. In this respect, writing as well as speech are the outward symbols of a nation.[67]

The phonetical, morphological and syntactical differences have further increased under the influence of the lexicon, which was formed separately in the two languages and which is generally derived from the higher levels of civilisation[68], scientific and technical terminology in modern times[69], word-formation under the influence of heterogeneous civilisations (West European (Roman Catholic)—East European (Orthodox Christian))[70] and very substantial borrowing from Russian among the Serbs and from German and Czech among the Croats.

Finally, it is hardly necessary to recall that the territory of Yugoslavia has for many centuries been a particularly significant meeting-ground for great historical, religious and artistic movements. Here were the frontiers, often unrecognised, between Byzantium and Rome, of the Greco-Byzantine culture and the Romano-Germanic civilisations. At the "meeting-point" of the two great branches of Christianity lies the Moslem world. Throughout the Middle Ages Roman Catholic Croats were subjected to Latin-Mediterranean, and later Central European influences. In this respect Vladimir

Vratović writes: "By Mediterranean relevance for Croatian culture and literature in particular, I primarily understand the influence of the Latin language and Roman literature, European Neo-Latin literature and partly (the direct or indirect impact of) Italian literature, and, of course, the entire Croatian spiritual climate and language that has been created along the Adriatic coast through the centuries. . . . It should not be surprising that I also deem it absolutely justified to introduce into the notion of the Mediterranean constant the Croatian language, its autonomous features and its expressive potential in literature". (*Croatian Latinity in the Context of Croatian and European Literature*, in Comparative Studies in Croatian Literature, pp. 63-79).

During the same period, the Orthodox Serbs were more receptive to Byzantine, and later to Russian cultural traditions. It would be surprising, in view of the cultural and religious division in Yugoslavia between Croats and Serbs, if their idioms had not developed differently.

It is the study of vocabulary which leads to the best understanding of the repercussions of historical and social events on the language, for words have an historical dimension. In fact, not only words but sentences too are laden with history, since "language is a supra-individual cultural product, the heritage of past generations", and it is history which prepares the synchronic functioning of a language. A literary language reflects, in itself, the riches of the past and to ignore its historical depth is to deal falsely, since the development of any koiné is usually connected with the history of the community by which it is used.

Four historical events encouraged the renewal and marked the evolution of the traditional Croatian vocabulary. First, the spread of Latin liturgy after the Synod of Split in 1060, which abolished religious services in Slavonic and replaced it with Latin. This event introduced a new contingent of Latinisms and drove out part of the Slavonic vocabulary. Later there was the Ottoman (Osmanli) invasion of Bosnia in the second part of the fifteenth century which opened the age of Turkish influence and Islamic civilisation in Bosnia. Finally, the

Venetian conquests in Dalmatia, starting in the twelfth century and continuing until the eighteenth century, and Austrian domination from 1527 to 1914 in the North of the country which opened the way to Italian and Germanic influences that have left a deep imprint upon the Croatian language. In Croatia the impact of the Latin-Catholic culture—mainly through contact with Italy and Austria-Hungary—was paramount.

The beginning of Croat civilisation does not coincide with the use of the Croat language proper. Croat culture has its roots in a tradition which was already national even if it was expressed in Latin. The historical fact that classical Latin was the habitual language of all Croatian writers and scholars from the Middle Ages to the nineteenth century is highly important to the history of the Croatian literary language. In general the clerics and educated men who communicated with each other through the medium of Latin (being bilingual) introduced a great many Latinisms into their Croatian writings. However, the bulk of the borrowings was not direct transfer but translation and imitation of single words. From Marulić (*De institutione bene beateque vivendi per exempla sanctorum*, Venice, 1506) to the Illyrians, nearly all Croatian writers wrote indiscriminately in Croatian or Latin.[71] Even today some poets, like Ton Smerdel and Nikola Šop, have written verses in Latin as well as in Croatian.

It should also be noted that Latin was the official language of the Croatian Diet, the *Sabor*, until 1847, replaced in 1848 by Croatian which thus became the language of State administration in Northern Croatia. Latin has thereby had a profound influence on Croatian. It has provided Croatian with abstract words: terms to express general ideas; a model for sentences designed to express complicated or delicate thoughts, and figures of speech modelled on the Latin. Thus the influence of Latin syntax on Croatian syntax is discernible until the end of the nineteenth century. In this respect Vladimir Vratović writes: "For in the Croatian language the influence of Latin as an important constituent factor is strongly felt, particularly in its syntax. When a full account of the history of the Croatian language is written one day, an account free of any romantic enthusiasm and freed of some basic mistaken notions—to which we are still to this day paying tribute—then this fact will become obvious. We will also see that the influence of Latin appears not only in the štokavian dialect, but also in kajkavian and čakavian. Thereby some deeper links between the three dialects will come to light in a historical perspective, thanks to a better understanding of their relationship to the Latin language whose elements from Antiquity or from contemporary Latin literature these three dialects adopted. . . . The Croatian writer, whether he created in both Latin and Croatian or only in Croatian, whether he belonged to the Croatian South or North, had for centuries been under the constant influence of the meaning and the shape of the Latin phrase, which was sanctified by tradition. He has always measured his Latin against the model of the Latin language of Ancient Rome and his Croatian against the model of Roman and contemporary European Latinity". (*Croatian Latinity in the Context of Croatian and European Literature, in Comparative Studies in Croatian Literature*, 63-79).

Furthermore, it was through Latin, preserved as the liturgical language throughout the Catholic world (and, until modern times, as the language of philosophy and science throughout Western Europe), that Croatian came under the strong influence of Western civilisation and formed a vocabulary capable of expressing all the essential ideas of that civilisation. If the unity of civilisation implies a unity of religion, it was through the Latin language and the Roman Catholic religion that Croat experienced the strong influence of Western civilisation.

At this point one ought recall that in 1102 Croatia entered into a political union with the Kingdom of Hungary which was to last until the battle of Mohacs (1526) when the Turks defeated the Hungarians and occupied much of the Croatian lands (Slavonia). This union was based on a treaty (*Pacta conventa*) whereby the Croats, following a military defeat at the hands of the Hungarians, agreed to accept the Hungarian King but retained a considerable measure of internal autonomy.

The Croats preserved their basic tradition and national assemblies were called to settle important matters though their political state was henceforth drawn into the affairs of Central Europe. From 1526 both the Hungarian and Croatian and also the Bohemian Kingdoms became united with Austria under the Habsburg dynasty. In 1867, following the establishment of the Dual Monarchy, Croatia came within the Hungarian kingdom once more, leaving Dalmatia to Austria. A prolongued linguistic contact between the two communities accounts for a number of words of Hungarian origin used in Croat, e.g. *baršun* 'velvet', *cipela* 'shoe', *čipka* 'lace', *čopor* 'a herd', *dobrac* 'measles', *gazda* 'master', *gulaš* 'goulash', *gumb* 'button', *karika* 'link of a chain', *kip* 'statue', *korov* 'weed = plant growing wild', *korteš* ' a canvasser', *lopov* 'thief', *orijaš* 'giant', *prsluk* 'waistcoat', *ruda* 'ore', *šogor* 'brother-in-law', *soba* 'room', *vrganj* 'champignon = mushroom', etc.

Loanwords are a rough and ready index of the degree of contact between two linguistic communities. Although the Croatian and Hungarian literary languages differ both genetically and typologically, to some extent they shared a similar historical fate.[72]

From the second half of the fifteenth century Croatian was also influenced by the Turkish language and Moslem culture. The Turkish conquest of Bosnia (1463) and Herzegovina (1482) and the subsequent Islamisation of the Bosnian population was highly important in the evolution of literary language in Bosnia. The Turkish superstratum has left an indelible imprint (particularly in the suffixes *-džija, -ana, -luk*) upon the popular speech of Bosnia, not only among Moslems but also among Christians. Furthermore, since Classical Arabic is the liturgical language of Moslems, the reading of verses from the Koran in the mosques has led to the introduction of a certain number of Arabic words. A great many words and idioms of Turkish, Arabic and Persian origin have been in common use in Bosnia and Herzegovina. The early literary style also made full use of such borrowings. With the development and under the influence of standard Croat, especially since 1878 when Turkey was obliged to withdraw from Bosnia, words and phrases of

63

Turkish origin have been falling out of use in everyday speech. Needless to say, even today, the spoken language in Bosnia as well as the literary language is deeply permeated with Turkish and Arabic terms which both give a special colour of their own.[73] It is sufficient to read any work by a Bosnian writer, such as Safvet-Beg Bašagić, Musa-Ćazim Čatić, Hasan Kikić, Alija Nametak, Enver Čolaković, Salih Alić, Ahmed Muradbegović, Mustafa Grabčanović, Šemsudin Sarajlić, Hamid Dizdar, Hifzi Bjelevac, Rasim Filipović, Elhem Mulabdić, Husein Muradbegović or Mak Dizdar to realise this.

ALJAMIADO[74]

It must also be noted that during a whole period from the seventeenth to the twentieth centuries some Moslem writers in Bosnia wrote their Croatian literary texts in Arabic characters. They used the letters of classical Arabic partly for different Croatian phonemes, but they also had to use additional letters and modifications of basic Arabic letters to express phonemes not found in Arabic. The orthography of Croatian written in Arabic was modelled on Turkish orthography. Parallel to the Catholic literature of Bosnian Franciscans, this aljamiado literature of Bosnian Moslems is written in *što* (*šća*)-*i*- dialect with a large admixture of Turkish, Arabic and Persian words and traits. It is a cultural hybrid which arose during Turkish rule in Bosnia, beginning in the second part of the sixteenth century and lasting until the end of the nineteenth century. It comprises, in general, poetical works of a religious or legal nature, usually didactic in tone, and a few works in prose (chronicle and fiction). There were a number of *aljamiado* poets who wrote religious poems, *ilahije*, moralo-didactic *kaside* and petitions (*mahzari*) or addresses (*arzuhali*) in the spirit of old Islamic traditions.

Of the devotional poetry 'worthy of note' are the poems in praise of the birth of Muhammed (*mewlud*). Of all datable *aljamiado* secular manuscripts the earliest text is the love romance *Chirvat-türkisi* (*Croatian song*) written c. 1588/89 in Erdel (Transylvania) by a certain Mehmed. In general,

Moslem folk poetry in Bosnia is reputed for its love poems (*sevda-linke*) and ballads (e.g. *Hasanaginica*) and nineteenth-century *aljamiado* poets were greatly influenced by folk poetry. The most outstanding author of *aljamiado* literature is the seventeenth-century poet Muhamed Havājī Uskūfī (1601-1651?) from Tuzla. He also compiled the first Turkish-Croat dictionary *Makbuli-arif* (1631) known as *Potur-šahidija* and written in Turkish verses.[75] Chronologically it is the second dictionary of the Croat language, Vrančić's *Dictionarium Quinque Nobilissimarum Europae Linguarum* (Venice, 1595) being the first if we exclude Lupis Valentiano's *Opera Nouva che insegna a parlare la lingua schiavonesca alli grandi, alli piccoli e alle done* (Ancona, ?1527).[76] As many Croat Roman Catholic writers from the fifteenth to the eighteenth centuries wrote both in Latin and Croat, Moslem writers in Bosnia at the same time wrote both in Croat and in oriental languages, mainly in Turkish, to a lesser extent in Persian and in a few instances in Arabic.[77] Altogether, more than a hundred poets wrote in these oriental languages up to the very end of the nineteenth century. Furthermore, the fact that Croatian was regarded, as early as the sixteenth century, as one of the diplomatic languages of the Ottoman Empire, proves the great influence of Bosnian Moslems in that Empire.[78] One of the best sources of information on the status of the Croatian language in the sixteenth century Turkish Empire is provided by the book *Itinerario di Marc'Antonio Pigafetta gentil'huomo Vicentino*, (141 p.), dedicated to Illustrissimo Signore Eduardo Seymer Conte d'Hertford and published in London in 1585 by John Wolf. In his travelogue Pigafetta describes the journey of two emissaries of the Austrian emperor Maximilian II (1527-1576) to the Sultan of the Turkish Empire in Constantinople. The emissaries and their retinue, of which Pigafetta was a member, left Vienna on 1st July 1567. The head of the delegation was the senior ambassador Antun Vrančić (1504-1573), a distinguished clergyman and scholar of Croatian descent and the uncle of the lexicographer Faust Vrančić.

Pigafetta writes that on their arrival in Buda, they paid their respect to the Pasha of Buda who received them in a very large stately hall "called by the Turks Divan, that is to say a council chamber." (p. 18); and then proceeds: "Although if they [the ambassador and the Pasha] had wanted, they could have spoken to each other in Croatian, however, the Pasha, for greater propriety and for many other reasons, desired the proposition to be put to him in Turkish. . . . And this was always done in the same way in Constantinople, except that in more private discourses of less importance or in some digressions, they [the Turks and the emissaries] would speak without interpreters in the Croatian language, which is familiar to nearly all the Turks and especially to the men of war." (p.19)

Some other sixteenth century documents and records attest the use of the Croatian language in the Turkish empire, especially in military administration and diplomatic relations with Central European Empires. Thus on 27 August 1553, the Great Vizier Rustem Pasha spoke in the Croatian language with the ambassadors of the Austrian Emperor Ferdinand I (cf. *Actio Antonii Verancii, Francisci Zay et Joannis Mariae Malvezzi oratorum . . . . apud principem Turcarum anno 1553 mense Augusto,* in: Monumenta Hungariae Historica; Scriptores IV, pars II, vol. 4 (Pest, 1858), 66).

On 29 September 1589 the representative of the Bosnian commander drew up a protocol in the Croatian and Turkish languages with the Venitian general commander in Dalmatia and Albania (". . . *zato mi rečeni Hodaveri čauš hotismo učiniti viru od toga posla i dvoje knjige pisati turske a dvoje Horvatske, rukom Ali ćehaja."*—in: Starine Jugoslavenske Akademije, X, 15 sq.).

Many outstanding Bosnian Moslems, who became public officials and military commanders in the Ottoman Empire in the 15th and 16th centuries, introduced the Croatian language as a contact vernacular in the Turkish Empire. (Cf. Safvet-beg Bašagić, *Znameniti Hrvati Bošnjaci i Hercegovci u turskoj carevini,* Zagreb 1931; id. *Bošnjaci i Hercegovci u islamskoj književnosti,* in: Glasnik Zemaljskog muzeja u Bosni i Hercegovini, 1912, 1-88, 295-390).

اورۇباق ožujak, تراون travan ili travanj, اسـویـبان isviban ili isvibanj, لیـپان lipan ili lipanj, سریان srpan ili srpanj, قولوووز kolovoz, روبان rujan, لیستوباد listopad, ستودنی studeni, پروسیناچ prosinac, سیهجان siječan ili siječanj, وألجه veljča ili velječa.

Croatian month-names from a Turkish 17th century calendar (1105/1693)
written in Arabic script.

As early as AD 1677 Turkey took over the solar (Julian) year with its month-names but kept the Muslim Era, computed from the starting point of the year of emigration (Hegira). March 1 was taken as the beginning of the year and thus the Croat name for March *ožujak* (*lažek*) is to be found in the Turkish calendars , commonly used in Bosnia by Muslims, as the first month of the year (cf. Fehim Spaho, *Naši narodni nazivi mjeseci u turskim kalendarima iz sedamnaestog vijeka,* in: Glasnik Zemaljskog muzeja u Bosni i Hercegovini, XLII, Sarajevo 1930, 185-204).

The title-page of *The Prayers of St. Brigit*, printed in Bosnian Cyrillic (Venice, 1512)

67

Another fact of civilisation and linguistics which is important for the history of the vocabulary of the Croatian literary language is the phenomenon of the Croatian-Italian or Croatian-German bilingualism of Croatian writers over the centuries. Thus, Dalmatian writers since the Renaissance have used two idioms concurrently, Croatian and Italian, while those of North Croatia used Croatian and German. The influence of these two languages on Croatian has been long and persistent, which explains the great many Italian borrowings in Dalmatia and German borrowings in the North, as well as turns of phrase modelled on Italian or German and transposed into Croatian.[79] With these two languages a certain intellectual affinity and community of culture have been created.[80] In this respect it is worth mentioning the testimony of Alberto Fortis, a well-known figure in the Age of Enlightenment, who in the Appendix to his famous book *Travels into Dalmatia* (London, 1778), after visiting the Croatian Littoral, writes: "The natural language of the country is Croatian; but all the genteel people of both sexes speak good Italian, and imitate the Tuscan manner. . ." (p. 510)

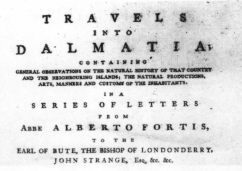

TRAVELS
INTO
DALMATIA;
CONTAINING
GENERAL OBSERVATIONS ON THE NATURAL HISTORY OF THAT COUNTRY
AND THE NEIGHBOURING ISLANDS; THE NATURAL PRODUCTIONS,
ARTS, MANNERS AND CUSTOMS OF THE INHABITANTS.
IN A
SERIES OF LETTERS
FROM
ABBE ALBERTO FORTIS,
TO THE
EARL OF BUTE, THE BISHOP OF LONDONDERRY,
JOHN STRANGE, Esq, &c. &c.

In the nineteenth century, at the time of Illyrianism a strong fear of Germanisation and Italianisation prevailed among Croats. By a reflex of linguistic defence, it was from the Czech language and, to a lesser extent, from Slovene[81], the other two Slavonic languages which form part of that single community of civilisation and cultural entity in Central Europe, that Croatian borrowed new terms to constitute a vocabulary capable of expressing new ideas arising out of the progress of science and the transformations of material civilisation. Let us mention a few words of Czech origin which entered the Croat language at that time and which were so well assimilated that only a philologist can tell their provenance, e.g. *dobrobit, dosljednost, gromada, gledište, kisik, klokan, listina, ljepenka, nakladnik, nazor, nesuvisli, odraz, ogavan, okolnost, opetovati, opstanak, osloviti, pisanka, pivovara, podneblje, podružnica, pojam, poprsje, prednost, primjeren, promjer, proslov, raslina, sadra, skladište, skromnost, skupina, slog, smjer, sob, tlak, uloga, ured, uspjeh, ustroj, uzor, uzoran* (*uzorit*), *veleban, vodik, zaraza, zastupnik, zbirka*, etc.

Slovene has provided literary Croat with a certain number of its calques, such as *ravnatelj* 'director', *nedužan* 'innocent', *blagostanje* 'well-being', *dugotrajan* 'lasting, enduring', *dalekovidan* 'far-sighted', (*razvoj* 'development'), *časnik* 'military officer' (semantic calque), *glasovir* 'piano', *spolovilo* 'sexual organ', etc. Consequently, lexical purism which played an important part in the process of Croatian lexical enrichment was to some extent mitigated by the wider Slavonic connexions of many of the new words. Thus Šulek in his Dictionary of Scientific Terminology (1874) recorded both the German calque *utisak* < *Eindruck* 'impression' and the Czech loanword *dojam* 'impression'.

As the language of any society is an integral part of its culture, many of the structural differences found in the vocabularies of Croatian and Serbian are to be accounted for in terms of cultural differences. Consequently, many Croat national institutional terms (i.e. political, administrative, legal, military and social terms) have varied from Serbian ones owing to differencies in social life and state organisation through the centuries. Thus the Croatian national diet is called *sabor* whereas the Serbian diet is *skupština*. Some of these Croatian national institutional terms are nowadays obsolete and are token-words (*mots témoins*, as French lexicologist Georges Matoré calls them) which evoke a fact of civilization and give the colour and flavour of a period. Although the words such as *ban, ceh, herceg, stališ, vlastela, vlastelin, vlastelinka, vla-*

69

stelinstvo, urbarij, kaštel, kaštelan, komornik, prepošt, špan, banski stol (tabula banalis), veliki župan, podžupan, varmeđa (< Hung. *vármegye*), *stožernik,* etc. are not currently used, they are to be found in the 19th and 20th century novels and are part and parcel of the Croatian lexical fund.

Many of these terms are political and designate an adherent or supporter of a person, a party or cause, such as the 19th century *ilirac, stekliš, mađaron, talijanaš, pravaš* and the 20th century *furtimaš, obzoraš, koalicionaš, frankovac, radićevac, mačekovac, ustaša.*

One has to analyse the common usage of these words in the contexts of the period, their temporal and social setting, to find out what they mean. Their meaning is socially-bound and cannot be abstracted from the historical forces and social matrix that have brought them into being. There are also military terms, some of which are very old, e.g. *satnik* (11th C.) 'centurion', *bojnik* (14th C.), *desetnik* (1578); others were created about the turn of the century: *domobran, domobranstvo, roj, čarkar,* etc. (cf. Toth-Schweitzer-Špicer, *Vojnički rječnik, hrvatsko-magjarski dio,* 1903). Some of these terms were brought back into use during the short-lived Independent State of Croatia (1941-1945); such are *rojnik, satnik, bojnik* and administrative terms indicating officials like *tabornik, logornik, stožernik,* etc. After 1918 and especially after 1945 all the Croatian military terminology has been officially Serbianized, thus *vojarna* 'barracks', *zapovjedništvo, zapovjednik* 'commander', *streljivo* 'ammunition', *stožer* 'headquarters', *topništvo* 'artillery', *okidač* 'trigger', *pucnjava* 'firing', *izvidnica (ophodnja)* 'patrol', *pobočnik* 'adjutant', etc. have been replaced by *kasarna, komanda, komandant, municija, štab, artiljerija, obarač, paljba, patrola, ađutant,* etc.

There are also some legal terms, designating judicial institutions (law courts), e.g. *sudbeni stol, stol sedmorice, kotarski sud,* which are now obsolete as they were replaced by the Serbian equivalents *kasacioni sud, sreski sud,* after World War II when Serbian has become within Yugoslavia what the German sociolinguist Heinz Kloss calls *Verdrängesprache* (replacement language).[82] Thus the Croat word *kotar* 'district, department' was replaced in Bosnia and Herzegovina by the Serbian *srez*. By the same token, every *gradsko vijeće* 'town council' in Croatia was replaced by the Serbian equivalent *skupština grada*, and *gradski vijećnik* 'a town councillor' was replaced by *delegat skupštine grada* while *pučka škola* 'primary school' has become *osnovna škola* and *pučkoškolac* 'pupil' turned into *osnovac*, etc.

The results of this expedition in time are as illuminating as the expedition in space of a dialect fieldworker in a given geographical area.

Communication difficulties obviously arise when two peoples have different denotative meanings for a word, for example *slovenski* in Serbian means 'Slavic' whereas in Croatian it means 'Slovenian'. Such differences in usage, however, would soon become apparent and could be   overcome. Communication problems which are more insidious in that they are not so easily detectable, arise where the connotative meaning of a concept is not shared. An interesting example of this is provided by political, social and religious terms which arouse a whole complex of associated ideas and feelings and which have different communal connotations for Croatians from those they have for Serbians.

Further, "Every language possesses in every period its own particular lexical system. But the original character of each of these systems stands out clearly when they are confronted with each other. It is particularly interesting in this confrontation to compare closely related languages to one another, for it is precisely when there is a great resemblance of the lexical *material* that the individual *structural* features of different lexical systems must come out in bold relief. In this respect Slavic languages provide a field of research as practicable and as rewarding as any." (*Travaux du Cercle linguistique de Prague*, 1. *Les theses de 1929*, Chapter 8, *Problemes de méthodes de la lexicographie slave*).

The evolution of the Serbian language which forms part of the linguistic community of the Balkan world, has been quite different. From the end of the fourteenth century the Turkish occupation cut Serbia off from the Western world and, with the loss of political independence, cultural continuity was broken. Consequently, Humanism, the Renaissance, the Reformation, the Counter-Reformation and the Baroque period had no influence in Serbia. During the centuries of Turkish domination the cultural level dropped low and the literary language nearly went out of use. The many Turkish expressions which have entered into popular and literary language (cf. Stevan Sremac's novel *Ivkova Slava* or Bora Stanković's *Nečista Krv* (Teinted Blood)) bear witness to this long Turkish domination. Let us mention only a few out of hundreds of Balkan Turkisms (Turkish loan words) of Arabic, Persian, Greek or Albanian origin which appear in Serbian and sometimes also in other Balkan languages (Bulgarian, Macedonian, Rumanian, Macedo-Rumanian, Demotic Greek or Albanian).

Some words of Turkish origin used in literary Serbian:	Lexical equivalents used in literary Croatian
bakalin 'grocer'	*trgovac mješovitom robom, sitničar* (neologism)
bakalnica 'grocery'	*sitničarija*
bašta 'garden'	*vrt*
baštovan 'gardener'	*vrtlar*
berberin 'barber'	*brijač*
bešika 'cradle, cot'	*kolijevka, zipka*
biber 'pepper'	*papar*
boranija 'French beans'	*mahune*
buđ 'mould, must, mildew'	*plijes(an)*
bunar 'well'	*zdenac < studenac*
but 'animal thigh'	*stegno*
čakšire 'a kind of trousers'	*hlače*
čamovina 'fir-wood'	*jelovina*
čaršav 'a bed sheet'	*plahta, ponjava*
činija 'tureen'	*zdjela*
čivut (čifut) 'Jew'	*židov*

čorba 'soup'	*juha*
ćilibar 'amber'	*jantar*
ćebe 'blanket - a bed covering'	*gunj, pokrivač*
ćup 'a jug'	*vrč, zemljani lonac*
ćurak 'fur coat'	*kožuh*
ćurčija 'furrier'	*krznar*
drangulije 'trinkets'	*kramarija*
dugme 'a button'	*puce, gumb* < Hung. *gomb*
dželat 'hangman'	*krvnik*
džigerica (*crna*) 'liver' (food)	*jetra*
džin 'a giant'	*div, gorostas*
đon (*pendžeta*) 'underpart of a shoe, sole'	*potplat*
(cf. *pođoniti, pendžerisati* 'to sole'	*staviti novi potplat*
đubre 'dung, manure'	*gnoj, smeće*
veštačko đubrivo 'fertilizer'	*umjetno gnojivo*
azotno đubrivo	*dušično gnojivo*
fitilj 'wick'	*stijenj*
hošaf 'dry fruit'	*suho voće*
jorgan 'a quilt'	*poplun*
kačamak 'polenta'	*palenta, pura, žganci*
kaišar 'usurer'	*lihvar*
kaišarluk 'usury'	*lihva*
kama 'dagger'	*bodež*
kajmak 'cream'	*vrhnje*
kalauz 'skeleton-key'	*otpirač*
kalaj 'tin, pewter'	*kositar*
kaldrma 'pavement' 'cobbled road'	*pločnik, trotoar* *tarac*
kalem 'reel'	*zavojnica*
kasapin 'butcher'	*mesar*
kašika 'a spoon'	*žlica*
kazan 'couldron'	*kotao*

kreč 'lime, limestone'	*vapno*
krečnjak 'limestone'	*vapnenac*
kirija 'a rent'	*najam, stanarina*
košava 'bora = cold north-east wind'	*bura*
kuluk 'corvee'	*tlaka*
lala 'tulip'	*tulipan*
lenger 'anchor'	*sidro, ankora*
marama 'scarf'	*rubac*
maramica 'handkerchief'	*rupčić*
makaze 'a pair of scissors'	*škare, nožice*
oklagija 'rolling pin'	*razvijač*
mamuza 'a spur'	*ostruga*
minđuša 'earring'	*naušnica*
odžak 'chimney'	*dimnjak*
okagača 'cross-beam'	*poprečna greda*
pače 'aspic'	*hladetina*
parčence 'a trifle'	*trunak*
peškir 'towel'	*ručnik*
rende 'a plane (tool)'	*blanja*
sirće 'vinegar'	*ocat, kvasina*
sunđer 'a sponge'	*spužva*
škembe '(cul.) tripe'	*fileki*
tabak 'sheet of paper'	*arak*
talas 'wave'	*val*
tapija 'deed book'	*gruntovnica, katastar*
terazije 'scales'	*vaga*
testija 'jug'	*vrč*
učkur 'waist-band'	*svitnjak*
ugursuz 'rogue, wag'	*vragoljan*
urma 'date (fruit)'	*datulja*
uzapćenje 'distress (leg.), seizure'	*ovrha*

zejtin 'edible oil'   *ulje*
etc.

The productive suffix -*če* used in Serbian to form diminutives is of Turkish origin; e.g. *lonče* 'small pot' Cr. *lončić, jastuče* 'cushion' Cr. *jastučić*, etc.

It is largely due to its autocephalous Orthodox Church that the Serbian people has preserved its national heritage. For centuries the Church has been a special guardian of Serbian culture and Orthodoxy became a codetermining element of national identiy. Church Slavonic, used as a liturgical and literary language, and to a lesser extent, Greek, were to the Serbs what Latin was to the Croats.[83]

The vestiges of the influence of Church Slavonic are perceptible in the contemporary Serbian language. Thus the group -*št*- in the words *opšti*, 'common', *uopšte* 'in general', *opština* 'a commune', *sveštenik* 'a priest', *mošti* 'relics of a saint' comes from Church Slavonic, the Croatian equivalents being *opći, uopće, općina, svećenik, moći*.[84]

The Serbian prefixes *protivu-, sa-* and *vaz-*, used in compounds are also of Church Slavonic origin. For example:

Serbian	Croatian
protivmera 'countermeasure'	*protumjera*
protivnapad 'counterattack'	*protunapadaj*
protiv(u)rečan contradictive	*protuslovan*, etc.
sabesednik 'interlocutor'	*sugovornik*
sadejstvo 'cooperation'	*suradnja*
saradnja 'collaboration'	
saosećaj 'sympathy'	*suosjećaj*
saputnik 'fellow traveller'	*suputnik*, etc.
vaspitati 'to educate'	*odgojiti*
vaspitanje 'education' (Cf. *fizičko vaspitanje* 'physical education'	*odgoj* *tjelesni odgoj*)
vaspitač 'educator'	*odgojitelj*, etc.

The influence of Church Slavonic on Serbian is particularly marked in vocabulary. For instance:

Serbian	Croatian
azbuka 'alphabet'	*abeceda*
beznadežan 'hopeless'	*beznadan*
bukvar 'primer'	*početnica*
čas 'hour'	*sat*
(Cf. *časovnik* 'a watch'	*sat, ura*)
Jevrejin 'Jew'	*Židov*
gojazan 'fat'	*debeo*
pol 'sex'	*spol*
polan 'sexual'	*spolan*
povinovati se 'to submit'	*pokoriti se*
prisustvo 'presence'	*prisutnost*
prasa (praziluk) 'leek'	*poriluk* < Ital. *porro*
(Old Church Slavonic Balkan Hellenism)	
prgav 'quick tempered'	*žustar, gnjevljiv*
prevazići (prevazilaziti) 'to surpass'	*nadmašiti, premašiti, nadići*
prodavac 'seller'	*prodavač*
prijatan (adj.) 'pleasant'	*ugodan*
sačiniti 'to make'	*načiniti, stvoriti*
sagledati 'comprehend'	*uočiti, shvatiti*
sahrana 'burial, funeral'	*ukop, pogreb, sprovod*
sopstven (adj.) 'proper, own'	*vlastit*
sopstvenik 'owner'	*vlasnik*
stihija 'natural force'	*prirodna sila*
(Old Church Slavonic Hellenism)	
snabdeti 'to supply'	*opskrbiti*
stub 'post'	*stup*
sudija 'judge'	*sudac*
suštastvo 'essence'	*bit(nost)*

sušti 'mere, sheer'	*pravi, puki*
trezven 'sober'	*trijezan*
ubica 'murderer'	*ubojica*
ubistvo 'murder'	*ubojstvo, umorstvo*
vajati 'to mould'	*oblikovati, klesati*
vajar 'sculptor'	*kipar*
u magnovenju 'in a jiffy'	*u tren oka*
vasiona 'cosmos'	*svemir*
vazduh 'air'	*zrak*
vazdušast 'airy'	*zračan*
— and the modern derivatives:	
vazduhoplov 'air-craft'	*zrakoplov*
vazduhoplovstvo 'aviation'	*zrakoplovstvo*
vazduhoplovni (adj.)	*zrakoplovni*
(Cf. *protivvazdušna odbrana* 'air defence'	*protuzračna obrana*)
Jugoslovenski vazdušni saobraćaj	*Jugoslavenski zračni promet*

Religious divergence between Roman Catholic Croats and Greek Orthodox Serbs bred simultaneously linguistic divergence. A great number of religious terms could be cited which are peculiar to Serbian Orthodox terminology and unknown to Croats, just as many terms could be cited which are special to the Catholic religion and unknown to the Orthodox world. For instance:

Serbian	Croatian
arhimandrit(a) 'abbot'	*opat*
blagodarenje 'thanksgiving'	*zahvala, misa zahvalnica*
Cvetonosije (Cveti) 'Palm Sunday'	*Cvjetnica*
crkvena riznica 'sacristy'	*sakristija*
činodejstvovati 'to celebrate'	*celebrirati, služiti misu*
činodejstvovanje 'liturgy'	*celebracija*
ćivot (kivot) 'reliquary'	*škrinja, moćnik*

77

Časni (Veliki) post 'Lent'	*Korizma*
diskos (nafornjak) 'paten'	*patena, plitica*
hleb naš nasušni 'our daily bread'	*kruh naš svagdanji*
iguman 'prior'	*prior*
iskušenje 'temptation'	*napast*
kaluđer (monah) 'monk'	*redovnik, fratar*
kaluđerica (monahinja) 'nun'	*redovnica, časna sestra, koludrica, duvna*
liturđija 'mass'	*misa*
manastir 'monastery'	*samostan, kloštar*
miropomazanje 'confirmation'	*potvrda*
nadežda 'hope'	*nada, ufanje*
nastojatelj 'principal, master'	*nadstojnik*
odežda 'chasuble'	*kazula, misnica*
skrnavljenje 'profanation'	*oskvrnuće*
osvetiti (osveštati) 'to consecrate'	*posvetiti*
ovaplotiti 'to incarnate'	*utjeloviti*
ovaploćenje 'incarnation'	*utjelovljenje*
pamjat 'requiescat'	*pokoj*
(Cf. *vječnaja pamjat* 'requiescat in pace aeterna'	*pokoj vječni,* *počivao u miru*
pomen 'service for the dead'	*zadušnica*
parastos 'requiem mass'	*zadušnice*
paroh 'parish priest, vicar'	*župnik*
parohija 'parish'	*župa*
pojac 'precentor'	*kantor (ckrveni pjevač)*
poslednje miropomazanje 'extreme unction'	*zadnja (posljednja) pomast*
protoiguman 'provincial'	*provincijal*
rukopoložiti 'to ordain'	*zarediti*
rukopoloženje 'ordination'	*(za)ređenje*
saborna crkva 'cathedral'	*stolna crkva*

Strasna nedelja 'Holy Week, Passion Week'	*Veliki tjedan*
stradanje Hristovo 'Passion'	*muka Isusova*
strašni sud 'Last Judgement'	*posljednji sud, sudnji dan*
sujeveran 'superstitious'	*praznovjeran*
sveta tajna 'sacrament'	*sakramenat, otajstvo*
sveto miro 'chrism'	*krizma*
Tajna Večera 'Last Supper'	*Posljednja Večera*
Trojice 'Pentecost'	*Duhovi*
tipik 'ordo'	*obraz (obraznik)*
Uspenje 'Assumption'	*Uznesenje (Marijino)*
vjeruju 'creed, credo'	*kredo, vjerovanje*
vladika (episkop) 'bishop' *eparh*.	*biskup*
vaskrsnuti 'to resurrect'	*uskrsnuti*
Vaskresenje 'Easter'	*Uskrs*
Voznesenje 'Ascension (Day)'	*Uzašašće, etc., etc.*

As the Serbs grew more nationally conscious, they became more Russophile, and later, in the nineteenth century, literary Serbian, promoted to the dignity of national language, came under the strong influence of the Russian language which belonged to the same community of civilisation constituted by the Orthodox world. Thus, many Russianisms penetratred into Serbian in the eighteenth century and later.

Some words of Russian origin used in literary Serbian	Lexical equivalents used in literary Croatian
Substantives	
ajkula 'shark'	*morski pas*
bekstvo 'flight'	*bijeg*
bezbednost 'security'	*sigurnost*
delovodnik 'protocol'	*urudžbeni zapisnik*
dejstvo 'effect, action'	*djelovanje, učinak*

gnušanje 'nausea, loathing'	*gađenje*
islednik 'investigator'	*istražitelj*
(Cf. *isledni sudija* 'an investigative judge'	*sudac istražitelj*)
konjica 'cavalry'	*konjaništvo*
lice 'person'	*osoba*
naravoučenje 'a moral lesson'	*pouka*
nauka 'science'	*znanost*
negodovanje 'dissatisfaction'	*nezadovoljstvo*
nužnik 'toilet'	*zahod*
obezbeđenje 'safety, security'	*osiguranje*
odstojanje 'distance between two objects'	*razmak, udaljenost*
odsustvo 'soldier's leave'	*dopust*
ophođenje 'dealing, conduct'	*općenje*
opit 'experiment'	*pokus*
osobenost 'particularity'	*osobitost, vlastitost*
otpravnik poslova 'chargé d'affaires'	*vršilac dužnosti*
podozrenje 'suspicion'	*sumnja*
podozrivost 'suspiciousness'	*sumnjičavost*
podrška 'support'	*potpora, pomoć*
podstrek 'encouragement'	*poticaj*
podvig 'great deed, exploit'	*pothvat*
poriv 'ardour, zeal'	*polet*
postrojenje 'establishment, plant'	*uređaj*
predostrožnost 'precaution'	*oprez, opreznost*
preimućstvo 'predominance, sway, advantage'	*prednost, povlastica*
prepiska 'correspondence'	*dopisivanje*
prezrenje 'contempt'	*prezir*
prijem 'reception'	*primanje*
prinuda 'compulsion, coercion'	*sila, prisila*

proizvoljnost 'self-will'	*samovolja*
prostota 'simplicity	*jednostavnost*
rastojanje 'distance'	*udaljenost, (raz)daljina*
rešenost 'decidedness'	*odlučnost*
rešenje 'decision'	*odluka*
saglasnost 'consent'	*pristanak*
samoopredelenje 'self-determination'	*samoodređenje*
saopštenje 'communication, notification'	*obavijest, priopćenje*
saučesnik 'participant'	*sudionik*
saučešće 'condolence'	*sućut*
sladostrasnik 'libertine'	*razbludnik*
spisak 'list'	*popis*
spisatelj 'writer'	*pisac*
srazmer(a) 'ration, proportion'	*omjer, razmjer*
staratelj 'guardian'	*skrbnik*
stepen 'grade'	*stupanj*
stremljenje 'aspiration, endeavour'	*težnja*
stroj 'formation (in army)'	*red*
sujeta 'vanity, conceit'	*taština*
telohranitelj 'bodyguard'	*čuvar, pratilac*
učesnik 'participant'	*sudionik, dionik*
učešće 'participation'	*sudjelovanje*
ushit 'enthusiasm'	*zanos*
uslov 'condition'	*uvjet*
uštrb 'damage'	*šteta*
vid 'form, aspect'	*oblik, lik*
vinovnik 'culprit'	*krivac*
zapeta 'comma'	*zarez*
zavesa 'curtain'	*zastor*
(*Cf. gvozdena zavesa* 'iron curtain'	*željezni zastor*)

81

Verbs

blagodariti 'to thank'	*zahvaljivati*
dejstvovati 'to act, to operate'	*djelovati*
gnušati se 'to be disgusted with'	*gaditi se*
isledovati 'to investigate'	*istraživati*
izjasniti se 'to take side'	*izjaviti*
iznuravati 'to exhaust'	*iscrpljivati*
izobličiti 'to expose (an impostor)'	*raskrinkati*
izviniti 'to pardon, excuse'	*oprostiti*
izvinjavati se 'to apologize'	*ispriča(va)ti se*
navodnjavati 'to irrigate'	*natapati*
obezbediti 'to secure, to get security'	*osigurati*
obezoružati 'to disarm'	*razoružati*
obnarodovati 'to proclaim, to announce publicly'	*objaviti, proglasiti*
oprovrgavati 'to belie'	*pobijati*
osporiti 'do dispute, to deny'	*pobiti, poreći*
osujetiti 'to baffle, to foil, to thwart'	*spriječiti, omesti*
otpravljati (poslove) 'to dispatch (affairs)'	*obavljati, izvršivati*
ozariti 'to cast light upon, to illuminate'	*obasjati*
podražavati 'to imitate'	*oponašati*
podstrekavati 'to instigate'	*poticati*
posmatrati 'to observe'	*motriti, promatrati*
podrazumevati 'to understand'	*razumijevati*
potčiniti 'to subjugate'	*podvrgnuti, podložiti*
preduprediti 'to prevent'	*spriječiti (doskočiti)*
prenebregavati 'to neglect'	*zanemarivati*
pretskazati 'to foretell'	*proreći*
prevazilaziti 'to surpass, outdo'	*nadilaziti, nadvisivati*

prevazići 'to surpass, to excel'	*nadmašiti, prevladati*
prinuditi 'to compel'	*prisiliti*
prisajediniti 'to annex'	*pripojiti, sjediniti*
rashodovati 'to enter expenses on books' (cf. *rashod, izdatak*)	*otpisati, uknjižiti izdatak*
razobličiti 'to unmask'	*raskrinkati, otkriti*
rešiti 'to decide'	*odlučiti*
saglasiti se 'to agree	*složiti se, pristati*
saobraziti 'to conform'	*uskladiti, prilagoditi*
sravnjivati 'to compare, to contrast'	*uspoređivati*
stremiti 'to strive' to aim at'	*težiti*
ubediti 'to convince'	*uvjeriti*
učestvovati 'to participate'	*sudjelovati*
upražnjavati 'to exercise, to perform'	*baviti se (čim)*
uprostiti 'to simplify'	*pojednostavniti*
usaglasiti (saglasiti se) 'to accord'	*uskladiti (složiti se)*
utoliti 'to quench (thirst)'	*utažiti* , etc.

Adjectives

blagorodan 'of noble birth'	*plemenit*
blagovremen 'timely'	*pravodoban*
blagozvučan 'harmonious'	*skladan*
bukvalan 'literal'	*doslovan, ropski, od riječi do riječi*
gord 'proud'	*ponosan, ohol*
izlišan 'superfluous'	*suvišan*
iznuren 'exhausted, washed-out'	*iscrpljen*
izvestan 'some, certain'	*neki, stanovit*
jednovremen 'simultaneous'	*istovremen*

83

ljubopitljiv 'curious, inquisitive'	*radoznao, znatiželjan*
nadležan 'competent, responsible'	*mjerodavan, kompetentan*
nedostupan 'stand-offish, aloof'	*nepristupačan*
neophodan 'indispensable'	*potreban*
neosporan 'indisputable'	*neprijeporan*
neposredan 'direct'	*izravan*
neprikosnoven 'inviolable, irreproachable'	*nepovrediv*
netrpeljiv 'intolerant'	*nesnošljiv*
neusiljen 'natural'	*prirodan, naravan*
osoben 'peculiar'	*osebujan, osobit*
podozriv 'suspicious'	*sumnjičav*
predostorožan 'cautious'	*oprezan*
prevashodan 'pre-eminent'	*pretežit, nadmoćan*
pribrežan 'coastal'	*obalni*
priležan 'diligent'	*marljiv, pomnjiv*
prinudan 'forced'	*prisilan*
pristrastan 'partial'	*pristran*
proizvoljan 'unsubstantial'	*samovoljan*
prost 'simple'	*jednostavan*
prostonarodan 'popular' (Cf. *prost narod* 'the common folk'	*pučki* *puk*)
rasejan 'absent-minded'	*rastresen*
ravnomeran 'uniform'	*podjednak, jednolik*
sebeljubiv 'self-centered'	*sebičan, samoživ*
snishodljiv 'considerate'	*podložan, susretljiv*
srazmeran 'proportional'	*razmjeran*
sujetan 'vain'	*tašt, isprazan*
sujeveran 'superstitious'	*praznovjeran*
surevnjiv 'envious'	*jalan, zavidan*

tečan 'fluid, liquid'	*tekući*
učtiv 'polite'	*uljudan*
uobražen 'conceited, vain'	*umišljen*
vispren 'agile'	*okretan, spretan*
volšeban 'magic, mysterious'	*čaroban, tajanstven*

The privative prefiz *bez-* 'non-, un-', indicating the lack or absence of something, used in literary Serbian in the formation of adjectives is of Russian or Church Slavonic origin; e.g.

bezbedan 'secure'	*siguran*
bezgraničan 'limitless'	*neograničen*
bezopasan 'harmless'	*neopasan*
bespomoćan 'helpless'	*nemoćan*
bespotreban 'unnecessary'	*nepotreban*
besprekidan 'continuous'	*neprekidan*
bespristras(t)an 'impartial'	*nepristran*

The considerable number of Russian adjectives which are to be found in Serbian confirms the theories of Gaston Paris that the influence of one language on another is particularly illustrated by the borrowings of adjectives. Obviously, this concerns the languages which possess the syntactic category of adjective.

At the same time many adjectives of Czech origin entered literary Croatian. Thus in Mažuranić-Užarević's dictionary *Njemačko-ilirski slovar* (1842) are recorded the folloving adjectives of Czech origin: *prvobitan, primjeran, dosljedan, gorljiv, nježan, udoban.* In Šulek's German-Croatian Dictionary (1860) are recorded *bajoslovan, dostatan, nedostatan, dotičan, drevan, ogavan, podal, stanovit, svjež, važan.*

In general the Croatian literary language of the nineteenth century is not receptive to foreign non-Slavic words. Haunted by the fear of losing their national identity, Croatian writers look for the equivalents of foreign words in the indigenous lexical stock and replace words of foreign origin with native coinages created by composition and derivation. They create the exact equivalents of foreign terms from the resources within the language alone. Compounds from native or naturalized words like *kišobran* 'umbrella', *vjetrobran* 'windscreen', *tlakomjer* 'barometer, manometer', *toplomjer* 'thermometer', *strujomjer* 'electrometer', *kutomjer* 'protractor' or *sladoled* 'icecream' have come into being with the things to which they refer, while *velevlast* 'great power', *veleizdaja* 'high treason', *veletrgovac (veletržac)* 'wholesaler' are calques from German *Grossmacht, Hochverrat, Grosshändler. Velegrad* 'metropolis' was taken from Czech; cf. Germ. *Grosstadt.*

Many of these Croatian coinages were later in the 20th century accepted by the Serbs to replace the foreign words: thus *sladoled* replaced in Serbian the Turkish *doldrma* and the German *gefrornes, kišobran* replaced *amrel, dvoboj* 'duel' replaced the Turkish word *megdan* and *olovka* 'pencil' replaced the German *plajvaz.* The 20th century Croatian coinage *podmornica* 'submarine' also replaced in Serbian *sumaren.*

Nineteenth century translators and popularizers of scientific works in Croatian often found the language deficient in technical terms for the subjects they wished to handle (medicine, natural sciences, philosophy and so on) and were obliged to invent new Croat words or expressions, e.g. *kolanje krvi* 'blood circulation', *raskužiti* 'to disinfect', *ošit* 'diaphragm', *zdravstvo* 'hygiene, sanitary measures', *upala* 'inflammation', *razina* 'level, niveau', *patvorenje* 'forgery, falsification', *krivotvoriti* 'to counterfeit', *hladetina* 'gelatine', *rastopina* '(chem.) solution', *plinara* 'gas-works', *rasvjeta* 'illumination', *raščlamba* 'analysis', *lučiti* (phil.) 'to discern', *rasuditi* (phil.) 'to discriminate, discern', *četvorina* 'square, quadrangle', *kazalo* 'index, register', *sitnozor* 'microscope', *tračnica* 'steel-rail', *pučanstvo* 'population', *pristojba* 'duty, fee, tax', *probitak* 'profit, advantage', *kovina* 'metal', *kušaljka* 'test tube', *zavojnica* 'spiral', *brojka* 'cypher', *proračun* 'budget', *mjernik* 'geometer', *brojnik* 'numerator', *ronilo* 'diving-bell', *zrcaliti se* 'to reflect light, to gliter, to shine', *oborina* < Germ. *Niederschlag* 'precipitation, rainfall', *paromlin (parni mlin)* < Germ. *Dampfmühle* 'steam-mill', *vjerovnik* < Germ. *Gläubiger* or Ital. *creditore* 'creditor', *podružnica* 'branch (business)', *sveučilište* < Lat. *universitas studiorum* (cf. Ital. *Università degli studi*), *žarište* 'focus', *slitina* 'alloy', *probava* 'digestion', *zrakoplovstvo* 'aeronautics', *propuh* (phys.) 'draught', etc. etc.

Interesting is Gaj's effort to introduce *-slovje*, after the Czech *-slovi*, as the equivalent of the Latin *-logia* > Germ. *-logie*; e.g. *rudoslovje* Ger. *Mineralogie*. The standard form *rudoslovlje* is recorded in Šulek's dictionaries. Šulek also recorded *mudroslovlje* 'philosophy', *zvjezdoslovlje* 'astrology', *krasoslovlje* 'belles lettres', which today are obsolete forms while *rodoslovlje* 'genealogy', *prirodoslovlje* 'natural science', *jezikoslovlje* 'philology', *bogoslovlje* 'theology, divinity' are still used. Another form *-slovija* is to be found in *bogoslovija* 'theology'

It was also from the Czech that Croats took over the formant *-pis* which corresponds to Latin *-graphia* and German *-beschreibung*, e.g. *životopis* < Cz. *životopis* 'biography' Lat. *biographia*, Germ. *Lebensbeschreibung*; *putopis* 'travelogue' Cz.*cestopis* Germ. *Reisebeschreibung*; *prirodopis* 'natural science' Gr. *Physiographie*. The formant *-pis* also translates the German *-schrift* as in *časopis* < Cz. *časopis* 'periodical' Gr. *Zeitschrift*; *rukopis* 'manuscript' Gr. *Handschrift, Manuscript*.

Literary Croat, on the whole, is full of coinages and neologisms obtained by compounding or derivation and in this respect differs from Serbian which uses a syntactic phrase or periphrasis, e.g.:

Croatian	Serbian
glasnice 'vocal cords'	*glasne žice*
razrednik 'form master'	*razredni starešina*
ubožnica 'alms-house'	*sirotinjski dom*
dragulj 'jewel'	*dragi kamen*
sunčanica 'sun-stroke'	*sunčani udar*
čitateljstvo 'the readers of a publication'	*čitalačka publika*
otajstvo 'sacrament'	*sveta tajna*

sastojina 'ingredient, a constituent element'	*sastavni deo*
porječje 'river basin'	*rečni sliv*
zubar 'dentist'	*zubni lekar*
pothodnik 'subway'	*podzemni prolaz za pešake*
ledište 'freezing point'	*tačka mržnjenja*
vrelište 'boiling-point'	*tačka ključanja*
talište 'melting point'	*tačka topljenja*
iskaznica 'identity card'	*lična karta*
pretinac 'letter box'	*sanduče za pisma*
spolovilo 'sexual organ'	*polni organ*
bubnjić 'ear-drum'	*bubna opna*
nekretnina 'real estate'	*nepokretna imovina*
hripavac 'whooping cough'	*veliki kašalj*
stotinka 'a hundredth'	*stoti deo*
njuh 'the sense of smell'	*čulo mirisa*
okus 'the sense of taste'	*čulo ukusa*
opip 'the sense of touch'	*čulo dodira*
potrbušnica 'peritoneum'	*trbušna maramica*
krletka 'bird-cage'	*kavez za pticu*
križaljka 'cross-word puzzle'	*ukrštene reči*
dvanaesnik 'duodenum'	*dvanaestopalačno crevo*
tiskanica 'printed matter'	*štampana stvar*
ronilo 'diving bell'	*gnjuračko zvono*
pisanica 'an Easter egg'	*uskršnje jaje*
slavoluk 'a triumphal arch'	*trijumfalna kapija*
pazikuća 'care-taker'	*nastojnik kuće*
poplućnica 'pleura'	*plućna marama*
trudovi 'labour pains'	*porođajni bolovi*
popravilište 'reformatory'	*zavod za vaspitanje mladih*
satnica 'school time-table'	*red nauka*
povećalo 'magnifying glass'	*uveličavajuće staklo*
osrčje 'coat of the heart'	*srčana kesa*, etc., etc.

This regeneration of the Croatian literary language by the traditional processes of lexical creation corresponds to a particular historical situation. The task was to create a vocabulary of culture capable of taking over from Latin and German, and the main suppliers of new terms are to be found among the scholars, the doctors, the economists and the technicians of all kinds, since the development of sciences and techniques has the inevitable corollary of the renovation of the vocabulary. The expansion of knowledge and the rise of the natural sciences inevitably led to word-formation. The disadvantage of words borrowed from Latin or Greek was that they were likely to be opaque to the reader lacking a classical education. For the same reasons the Croatian scholars draw upon the lexical fund of Croatian tradition to create new words from indigenous elements. They coin the lexical neologisms of scientific nomenclature modelled on foreign terms, mainly German, or borrow from the Czech. In brief, Croatian language loyalty and ethnic pride manifested itself in the nineteenth century against foreign, expecially German encroachment.

For the Serbs, who had their own Principality or Kingdom and were less threatened with absorption by German culture, this danger did not exist. That is why the Serbian literary language remained more open and tolerant of foreign borrowings than Croatian and it also explains why doublets and the binary nomenclature are used in Croatian: *sveučilište - univerzitet, glazba - muzika, djelotvoran - efikasan, tvornica - fabrika, momčad - tim, zemljopis - geografija, čimbenik - faktor, gospodarstvo - ekonomija, odvjetnik - advokat, skladba - kompozicija* (musical), *skladatelj - kompozitor, podružnica - filijala, mimohod - defile, sustav - sistem, oporba - opozicija, glavnica - kapital, mirovina - penzija,* etc.[85] By contrast, in Serbian, there are few loan-translations, foreign borrowings being used instead. It is peculiar to the Serbian and Croatian reform movements that Serbian was rather inclined to use foreign words while in Croatian innovations by inherent means prevailed, e.g. Serbian *šnicla* 'escalope' < German *Schnitzel* as opposed to Croatian *odrezak* < *od+rezak* 'cutting off'; Serbian *šporet* < German *Sparherd* 'kitchen-range' as opposed to Croatian *štednjak* (*štedjeti* = Germ. *sparen*). On this model was later formed *hladnjak* 'refrigerator' Germ. *Kühlschrank;* (cf. Serbian *paradajz* < German *Paradiesapfel* — Cr. *rajčica* (*raj* = Germ. *Paradies*)), Sb. *krofna* 'doughnut' < German-Austrian *Zwickkrapfen* — Cr. *uštipak*, Sb. *juvelir* 'jeweler' Cr. *draguljar*, Sb. *lenjir* 'ruler' Cr. *ravnalo*, Sb. *kragna* 'collar' Cr. *ovratnik*, Sb. *pegla* < Germ. *Bügeleisen* 'iron' Cr. *glačalo*, Sb. *pantalone* 'trousers' Cr. *hlače*, Sb. *bina* 'stage' Cr. *pozornica*, Sb. *pelcovati* 'vaccinate' Cr. *cijepiti*, Sb. *buter* 'butter' Cr. *maslac*, Sb. *kelner* 'waiter' Cr. *konobar*, Sb. *supa* 'soup' Cr. *juha*, Sb. *štrudla* 'strudel' Cr. *savijača*, Sb. *hibrid* 'hybrid' Cr. *križanac*, Sb. *cirkulacija* 'circulation' Cr. *kolanje*, Sb. *cirkular* 'circular (letter) Cr. *okružnica*, Sb. *karfiol* 'cauliflower' Cr. *cvjetača*, Sb. *braun* 'brown' Cr. *smeđ*, etc.

The impact of loan-translations was so strong that the native simple words such as *ratar* 'ploughman', *savjetnik* 'counsellor', *slap* 'waterfall', *vijek* 'century', etc. have been challenged by the compounds *zemljoradnik* < Ger. *Landarbeiter*, *savjetodavac* < Ger. *Ratgeber*, *vodopad* < Ger. *Wasserfall*, *stoljeće* < Ger. *Jahrhundert*, etc. In the same way the adverb *naime* < Germ. *nämlich* replaced the archaic Church Slavonic *bo*.

Serbian also possesses calques, but in a smaller number, e.g. *moreuz* 'straits' < G. *Meerenge* Cr. *tjesnac*, Sb. *zemljouz* 'isthmus' < G. *Landenge* Cr. *prevlaka*, Sb. *upijač* 'blotting paper' < Fr. *buvard* Cr. *bugačica*, Sb. *zmijski car* 'boa' < Ger. *Königsschlange* Cr. *udav*.

Even the proper names of persons of foreign origin, whether first names or surnames, have been translated into Croatian; thus *Florian* became *Cvjetko* (Lat. *flos* = Cr. *cvijet*), *Felix* became *Srećko* (Lat. *felix* = Cr. *sretan*), *Aurelija* > *Zlata*, *Adeodat* > *Bogdan*, *Agaton* > *Dobroslav*, *Anastazija* (*Flora*) > *Cvijeta*, *Eleuterije* > *Slobodan*, *Hilarije* > *Radovan*, *Telemah* > *Dalibor*, *Teofil* > *Bogoljub*, *Teodor* > *Bogoslav*. Very old Croat names *Miroslav* and *Dragutin* have been substituted for German *Friedrich* (Germ. *Friede* = Cr. *mir*) and *Karl*. German *Leopold* became *Lavoslav*, although *Leo-* is not the semantic equivalent of *Lav* 'lion' but represents an old *Liut-*

(old form *Liutpold*) of the same etymon as Modern German *Leute*.

The process of stabilization of surnames in Croatia occurred in the 15th and 16th centuries. However, as early as the 17th century foreign Christian and family names were often translated into Croat; for instance, the name *Ritter* of the 17th century historian and lexicographer *Pavao Ritter-Vitezović* (1652-1713) (Germ. *Ritter* = Cr. *Vitez*). It was especially in the 19th century that it became fashionable to Croatianize foreign names. Thus the 19th century Croat lexicographer and Italianist Karlo Parčić used to write his name in Italian *Carlo* and in Croat *Dragutin*. The latter form (*Dragutin*) being established by a far-fetched etymology of Lat. *carus* = Cr. *drag(i)* 'dear', hence Lat *Carolus* = Cr. *Dragutin*. The other 19th century lexicographer Rudolf Fröhlich Croatianized his name into *Veselić* (Germ. *fröhlich* = Cr. *veseo* 'joyful'). Some 19th century writers also kept two surnames, the foreign and Croatian; e.g. *Ferdo Livadić-Wiesner* (1788-1878) (Germ. *Wiese* = Cr. *livada* 'meadow'); *Ljudevit Farkaš-Vukotinović* (Hungarian *farkas* = Cr. *vuk* 'wolf'); *Adolf Veber-Tkalčević* (1825-1893) (Germ. *Weber* = Cr. *tkalac* 'weaver'). The famous linguist *Vatroslav Jagić* (1838-1923) originally baptized *Ignac*, translated his first name into *Ognjoslav*, then *Vatroslav* (Lat. *ignis* = Cr. *oganj, vatra*). His namesake *Vatroslav Lisinski* (1819-1854), the 19th century musician and composer, was originally called *Ignac Fuchs* (Germ. *Fuchs* = Cr. *Lisica*).[86]

Croatian thus belongs to the Western group of Slavonic languages, such as Slovene, Czech and Lusatian which »make wide use of the process of calque to create a literary language".[87] A consequence of it was a unification of the conceptual worlds of these languages, which came to reflect a similar view of reality, despite their superficial divergences.

The point to be made here is that the extension of the Croatian vocabulary by means of borrowing and the modification of the meaning of existing Croatian words and phrases by means of loan-translation (calque) have involved changes in the lexical structure of the language system.

Besides the convergence of the lexicons of European

languages caused by loan-words, there is another kind of convergence created by calques. The calques of words and phrases are numerous not only in Germanic and Slavonic languages, but also in Finno-Ugric languages (Hungarian, Estonian, Finnish). In addition to the conformities due to the borrowings which affect, at the same time, form and meaning, there is a whole series of correspondences due to calques which cause a parallelism to appear which is confined to meaning. It is the superimposition of these two types of phenomena, borrowing and calque, which make European languages easily translatable even if they are genetically or typologically unrelated.

After Vuk, Serbian writers and lexicographers (cf. D. Popović's *Rečnik srpskoga i nemačkoga jezika* I/II, Pančevo 1879/ 1881) admitted a considerable number of foreign, especially Russian, words into literary language without insisting on their replacement by calques. They approved the acceptance of such 'international' words into the lexicon of the newly literary language; generally speaking Serbian has continued to show much less strong tendencies towards purism, at least as far as Russianisms and internationalisms are concerned, than Croatian.

Thus, the Croats, at the time of their national revival, Illyrianism, constituted their vocabulary of modern civilisation separately, that is to say, in a spirit of national preservation and renovation. The Croats and the Serbs, therefore, found themselves also with distinct learned languages. Let us note, at random, only a few terms of building terminology which differ in the two languages. E.g.:

Croatian	Serbian
blanjati 'to plane'	*rendisati*
brtvljenje 'caulking'	*zaptivanje*
čavao 'nail'	*ekser*
kat 'storey, floor'	*sprat*
klesani kamen 'cut stone'	*tesani kamen*
kut 'angle'	*ugaonik*

kutna letvica 'skirting'	*nasatična daska*
ljepenka za izolaciju 'bitumenous felt damp-proofing'	*izolaciona hartija*
ljestve 'ladder, steps'	*merdevine*
obujam 'volume'	*obim*
okomica 'vertical (line)'	*vertikala*
omjer 'ratio'	*srazmera (razmera)*
otpadna cijev 'rain water down pipe'	*olučnjak*
petlje 'hinges' (*brtvjele, panti*)	*šarke* (*baglame*)
pila 'a saw'	*testera*
ploha 'level surface'	*ravan*
promjer 'diameter'	*prečnik*
pod 'floor'	*patos*
polumjer 'radius'	*poluprečnik*
pročelje 'façade'	*lice (kuće)*
rub 'edge'	*ivica*
sljubnica 'butt joint'	*sučeoni spoj*
strop 'ceiling'	*tavanica, plafon*
stubište 'staircase'	*stepenište*
čelične stube 'steel stairs'	*gvozdene stepenice*
ugao 'corner'	*ćošak*
umjetni mramor 'artificial marble'	*veštački mermer*
vapno 'lime'	*kreč*
vijak 'screw'	*zavrtanj*
vilice 'stirrups'	*uzengije*
žbuka (mort) 'mortar'	*malter*
žbukanje 'rendering, plastering'	*malterisanje*
žlijeb 'gutter'	*oluk* , etc.

One could also cite hundreds of terms from various sciences which differ in the two languages, such as the most common zoological terms. E.g.:

Croatian	Serbian
američki skočimiš 'dipodomys'	*kengurski pacov*
biljožder 'herbivore'	*biljojed*
čegrtuša 'rattle snake'	*zvečarka*
člankonožac 'arthropod'	*zglavkar*
deva 'camel'	*kamila*
dikobraz 'porcupine'	*bodljikavo prase*
dupin, pliskavica 'dolphin'	*delfin*
glavonožac 'cephalopod'	*desetoručac*
glodavac 'rodent'	*glodar*
grinje 'maggots'	*pregljevi*
gruj, grug 'conger'	*morska jegulja*
hrušt 'cock-chafer, may bug'	*gundelj*
kolutićavci 'annelides'	*prstenasti crvi*
klokan 'kangaroo'	*kengur*
kljova 'tusk'	*zub* (*slona, divljeg vepra*)
kornjaši 'coleoptera'	*tvrdokrilci*
kralješnjaci 'vertebrates'	*kičmenjaci*
kukac 'insect'	*buba, insekt*
kukcožder 'insectivore'	*bubojed(ac)*
ličinka 'larva, maggot'	*larva*
mješinci 'coelenterata'	*dupljari*
morž 'walrus'	*morski konj*
osa 'wasp'	*zolja*
pasanac 'armadillo'	*oklopnik*
papiga 'parrot'	*papagaj*
poskok 'vipera ammodytes'	*kamenjarka*
plijenor 'colymbus'	*morski gnjurac*
puran 'turkey cock'	*ćuran*

pura 'turkey'	*ćurka*
sisavac 'mammal'	*sisar*
sob 'reindeer'	*irvas*
svilac 'silk-worm'	*svilena buba*
svizac 'marmot'	*marmot*
šišmiš 'bat'	*slepi miš, ljiljak*
šojka 'jay'	*kreja*
štakor 'rat'	*pacov*
smeđi štakor 'rattus norvegicus'	*pacov selac*
šturak 'gryllus cricket'	*popac*
tobolčar 'marsupial'	*torbar*
trp 'holuthuria'	*morski krastavac*
trakavica 'tapeworm'	*pantljičara*
pasja trakavica 'taenia echinococcus'	*jetrena pantljičara*
tuljan 'seal'	*foka*
udav 'boa constrictor'	*boa, zmijski car*
urlikavac 'howling monkey'	*drekavac*
zlatna mara 'lady-bird'	*buba zlata*
zlatnice 'chrysomelidae'	*bube listare*
žličarka 'platalea leucorodia'	*kašikarka*
žohar (crni) 'cockroach'	*bubašvaba*
smeđi žohar 'blatella germanica'	*bubarusa*

etc., etc.

All this recent lexical superstructure has made a large contribution to the divergences between the two languages. It is these dissimilarities which give speakers as well as listeners the impression that there are really two quite different structures of communication, even if it is agreed to use the single term "Serbo-Croat" to indicate Serbian and Croatian idioms and to take a single linguistic basis for diachronics.[88] Being an umbrella name for the very similar Serbian and Croatian languages, the phrase 'the Serbo-Croat language' is itself highly misleading, for there is no such animal. It is not a single, homogeneous, stable entity: it is a complex mixture of varying structures. The term "Serbo-Croat" is merely a common denominator to designate a linguistic and grammatical phenomenon which is *sui generis*. By the mere fact of being a compound word, hyphenated or not, the term "Serbo-Croat" is ambiguous from the semantic point of view. As a spoken and written language, "classical Serbo-Croat", as Antoine Meillet called it, is only achieved in the writings of some philologists who breathed life into it and sustained the idea artificially without paying too much attention to the linguistic reality.[89] In the case of Croatian (*-i-je-*) and Serbian (*-e-*), they are languages spoken in adjoining regions which have been subject in the course of history to different influences with the final result that present-day Serbian and Croatian offer different aspects.

The differences between Serbian and Croatian concern the overall grammar; they relate primarily to the lexicon, which deals with the analysis of the vocabulary of the language and then, to a lesser extent, to the grammar proper, which deals with the analysis of the sentence. "In particular, it is not known whether there is a clear-cut psychological distinction to be drawn between grammar and lexicon. At any rate, linguists have so far found it impossible to draw any such distinction sharply in the description of particular languages."[90] In any case grammar cannot be restricted to phonology and syntax as being independent from lexicon and meaning, since a sentence could be grammatical without being meaningful just as the syntax might be right and the semantics wrong. Our knowledge of language includes more meaning than most have been willing to admit in their traditional concept of grammar. Grammar is only part of language and grammatical and lexical knowledge interact to create meanings.

In search for some common Serbo-Croat grammar, specific differences between Serbian and Croatian, requiring a realistic interpretation of linguistic competence and performance, have been overlooked. Although there are certain principles, properties and kinds of grammatical operation which are common to both of them, there are also obvious and varied differences in the outward forms of the two languages. If strictly necessary, we could consider "Serbo-Croat" as a dia-system with two distinctive linguistic norms which determine the standard form of two literary or national languages, Serbian and Croatian. Although two different literary and national standards, Serbian and Croatian, developed in the nineteenth century with which two communities still associate them-selves politically and culturally, the distinction between Serbian and Croatian as vernaculars, in terms of their structure, is another matter. Although the difference between the two standards is clear enough, there is a whole range of socially and geographically (Bosnia and Herzegovina, Montenegro) determined vernaculars linking them.

Even from the point of view of dialectical or historical mater-ialism, which proclaims that the accumulation of quantitative differences must be reflected in a new quality, we could speak of two structures since the quantitative differences between the two languages appear very substantial in certain contexts even if they are negligible or minimal in some others. [91]

But let us leave aside Hegelian dialectic, to note that in 1935 the Serbian philologist Radosav Bošković wrote that "the differential Croato-Serbian or Serbo-Croatian dictionary would contain three or four thousand words. And it does not seem to me that this number is a trifle". [92] In 1940 there ap-peared, published by Matica Hrvatska of Zagreb, a little dictionary, fairly incomplete, of the differences between literary Croatian and literary Serbian [93] , and we are now pro-mised the publication of an improved differential Serbo-Croat dictionary. The first dictionary had up to 4,000 words and the new one will have 10,000. [94] If we take into consideration the fact that the Slovak-Czech dictionary (Kalal (Kar.)—Salva (Kar.), *Slovnik slovenskočesky a československy*, Lipt. Ružom-berk, 1896) comprises 4,315 words which differ in two languages, the lexical differences between Croat and Serb seem to be even greater.

Throughout its history, literary Croatian has been subject to mutation which has taken many forms. Borrowing has occurred at all periods and continues today. New words have entered as the old words lapsed. Grammatical conventions have changed under pressure of idiomatic use or by cultural ordinance.

In the 19th century, Croat was acquisitive of lexical and grammatical innovation and discarded eroded units with conscious speed. Thus, for instance, the plural cases of feminine nouns ending in -a, such as *žena* 'woman', i.e. gen. pl. *ženah*, dat. *ženam*, loc. *ženah*, instr. *ženami* were simplified and reduced to gen. pl. *ženâ*, dat. loc. and instr. pl. *ženama*; the writing of the syllabic *r* without a glide-vowel, e.g. *prst* 'finger' instead of *perst* or *parst* also prevailed. In other instances, 19th-century literary Croatian was strongly conservative, preserved in an artificially static condition as is illustrated by the writings of Fran Kurelac (1811-1874) and the so-called Rijeka philological school.[95]

Compared to literary Serbian, literary Croatian is more conservative. Consequently, Croatian has preserved the Slavonic genitive; e.g. *Ne znam mu imena. Nije našao čestite djevojke. Nitko nije ćutio nevidljive studeni.* It has also preserved the predicative instrumental; e.g. *Hoćete li nam i dalje biti suradnikom? Postao je tvojim dijelom. Pamti kad je bio djetetom.*

In general, at most stages in the history of literary Croatian, innovative and conservative tendencies coexisted.

Some Developments in 20th Century
Croatian Vocabulary

In the twentieth century new words have continued to enter Croat from foreign languages and new coinages have been made. A genuine problem arises when changes in the lexicon can be largely accounted for by simple addition of items and relationship, or, less frequently, by the desuetude and loss of particular words. Loan words are the most immediately obvious and the most important or numerous additions to vocabulary. To mention only the languages from which Croat had already been borrowing for a long time, German and Czech were the source of many compounds and loan-translations in the nineteenth century and even earlier. Thus the borrowing *krvotok* 'bleeding', Ger. *Blutfluss*, Cz. *krvotok*, Pol. *krwotok*; and *ribolov* 'fishing', Ger. *Fischfang*, Cz. *rybolov* were recorded in eighteenth century dictionaries. Later in the nineteenth century the loan-translations *knjigovođa* 'book-keeper', Ger. *Buchführer*, and *poslovođa* 'manager', Ger. *Geschäftsführer*, were modelled on the native compound *kolovođa* 'ringleader', while *parobrod* 'steamboat', Ger. *Dampfschiff, paromlin* 'flour-mill', Ger. *Dampfmühle, vodovod* 'water conduit', Ger. *Wasserleitung*, and *vodopad* 'waterfall', Ger. *Wasserfall* were taken over from Czech. *Vodostaj* is a loan translation of Germ. *Wasserstand*.

This type of compounding which consists of placing next to each other two substantives, the first qualifying the second, is rare in Croat. In the twentieth century, foreign syntagmes, especially those borrowed from German, introduced this kind of compound of juxtaposed words, e.g. *zubotehničar* 'dental technician' Ger. *Zahntechniker, drvosječa* 'wood-chopper' Ger. *Holzhacker, kućepazitelj* 'caretaker' Ger. *Hausmeister* (cf. *pazikuća*). This type of composition tends to penetrate more and more technical and scientific terminology and from there to pass into current usage. Thus on the model of foreign com-

99

pounds *autogaraža* < Ger. *Autogarage*, *autokar* 'coach' < Fr. *auto-car*, *autostrada* 'motorway' < Ital *autostrada* have been coined words *auto-servis* 'petrol-station', *auto-cisterna* 'petrol tanker', *auto-put* 'motorway', *auto-škola* 'driving school'. One could also cite neologisms: *radio-prenos* 'transmission', *radio-emisija* 'broadcast' etc.; or agent-nouns: *strojoslagar* 'linotype compositor', *vodo-instalater* 'plumber', *krovopokrivač* 'tiler', *kovinotokar* 'metal turner', etc.

Usually the first word of the German coordinated compounds is rendered into Croatian by an attributive adjective, e.g. Ger. *Blutdruck* 'blood pressure' > Cr. *krvni tlak*, Ger. *Postfach* 'post box' > Cr. *poštanski pretinac*, *Kammermusik* 'chamber music' > Cr. *komorna glazba*, *Fischsuppe* 'fish soup' > Cr. *riblja juha*, Ger. *Eingabeprotokoll* 'minute book' > Cr. *urudžbeni zapisnik*.

On the other hand Croatian tends to expand the German compounds into descriptive phrase, with the help of added joining words such as prepositions (*za, u, na* etc.) e.g. *Esszeug* 'tableware' > Cr. *pribor za jelo*, *Bücherschrank* 'bookcase' > Cr. *ormar za knjige*, *Reithose* 'riding-breeches' > Cr. *hlače za jahanje*, *Staubzucker* 'castor sugar' > Cr. *šećer u prahu*, *Spiegelei* 'fried egg' > Cr. *jaje na oko*, etc.

However, Croatian contrasts with German in that creating new words by affixing is more common than that of compounding.[96] Therefore, there is a tendency in newly coined words to replace a German or a foreign compound by a single word; e.g. *ukosnica* 'a hairpin' Ger. *Haarnadel*, *stezaljka* '(screw) clamp' Ger. *Schraubenzwinge*, *sjenilo* 'a lamp-shade' Fr. *abat-jour* Ger. *Lampenschirm*, *sitničar* 'grocer' Ger. *Kleinhändler* cf. Fr. *détaillant*, *zvučnik* 'loudspeaker' Ger. *Lautsprecher* (cf. Serbian *glasnogovornik*), *kovinar* 'metallurgist' Ger. *Metallarbeiter*, *tuđica* 'foreign word' Ger. *Fremdwort*, *uzletište* 'airfield' Ger. *Flugplatz*, *Aufflugplatz*, *cjenik* 'price-list' Ger. *Preisliste*, *kupaonica* 'bathroom' Ger. *Badezimmer*, *staklenik* 'greenhouse' Ger. *Glashaus*, *grudnjak* 'brassiere' Ger. *Busenhalter*, *stolnjak* 'tablecloth' Ger. *Tischtuch*.

The more productive the affix which is used to form new words (neologisms), the more easily the neologisms are integrated. These two processes of compounding and affixation have remained the major sources of new words in Modern Croatian.

Whereas at the beginning of the twentieth century German borrowings and turns of phrases in literary Croat were avoided, in Serbian literature Germanisms like *špajz(a)* < Ger. *Speise, šlep* < Ger. *Schlepp-Dampfer, šporet* < Ger. *Sparherd, pegleraj* < Ger. *Büglerei, šnajderaj* < Ger. *Schneiderei, šlajfa/šlajf(na)* < Ger. *Schleife* etc. are often to be found. The neoštokavic purism of Croat philologists is manifest in the works of Nikola Andrić (*Branič jezika hrvatskoga*, Zagreb, 1911), Vatroslav Rožić (*Barbarizmi u hrvatskom jeziku*, Zagreb, 1904) and above all in Maretić's *Filologičko Iverje* or *Jezični Savjetnik*, Zagreb, 1924.

While still highly purist in comparison with Serbian, after World War II, literary Croat has become far more tolerant of foreign loan-words. The strictly purist attitudes of the Croatian 19th century revival period were modified, so that more loan-words were accepted in preference to calques; thus we can now speak of the internationalization of the Croat lexicon. During the Modern period, the vocabulary of Croat has continued to expand, and indeed at the present time the expansion seems to be going on at a pridigious rate. Contemporary Croat readily assimilates international words (terms); a Croatian purism, in spite of the excesses committed in the past, does not exist any longer. In the great majority of cases such international words derive from ancient Greek or Latin which have played the special role in the lexical development of European science and civilisation and in the convergence of the conceptual worlds reflected in them. As a consequence of the internationalization of Croat lexicon, many 19th century calques of foreign learned and technical terms have become obsolete and replaced by the foreign, international equivalents, thus *mudroslovlje* was ousted by *filozofija, rudoslovlje* by *mineralogija, tlakomjer* by *barometar, sitnozor* by *mikroskop, slovnica* by *gramatika*, etc. In this respect it is interesting to note that the German loanword *vâga* < *Wage* 'balance', which the 19th century lexicographer Šulek considered to be improper, ousted *tezulja*, and a short derivative *poštar* 'postman' ousted *listonoša* modelled on German *Briefträger* and Ital. *portalettere*.

However, there is no single answer to the question why some loan translations became obsolete; a number of factors may be involved: homophony (*rudoslovlje/rodoslovlje*), taboo, linguistic snobbism, taste for novelty, the impact of international scientific jargon, etc. Perhaps one of the most important factors is the tendency for words to fall into roughly synonymous pairs of which one is fashionable, markedly neologistic, the other unfashionable, treated as archaic or obsolescent. Consider *pejsaž/krajobraz* (*krajolik*), *inventar/našastar*, *epruveta/kušaljka*, *teleskop/zvjezdozor*, *arhiv/pismohrana*, *deklamirati* (*recitirati*)/*krasnosloviti*, *radius/šestar*, *teologija/bogoslovija*, *drama/igrokaz*, *telegram/brzojav*, *stenografija/brzopis*, etc.

It might be assumed that a loan word would normally be borrowed to make good a specific deficiency in a language. The above examples show that this is only partly true.

In the Independent State of Croatia (April 1941—May 1945), Croatian linguistic purism manifested itself again: new words were coined to replace international terms. Thus neologisms *brzoglas, krugoval, promičba, slikokaz* replaced *telefon, radio, propaganda, kino*. On the other hand, words coined in the 19th century, which fell out of use, were brought back into use and assumed new meanings to handle new ideas or objects; e.g. *samovoz* 'automobil', *slikopis* 'film', *svjetlopis* 'photography' etc. Similarly many military and political terms were brought back into use, such as *bojnik, čarkar, rojnik* (*roj*), *satnik* (*satnija*), *stožernik, tabornik, logornik*, etc. (cf. T. Toth — D. Schweitzer — M. Špicer, *Vojnički Rječnik* (*hrvatsko-magjarski dio*) (Croatian-Hungarian Dictionary of Military Terminology), Budapest, 1903, 574 p.).

Modern civilization demands a plethora of terminology and Croat obtains it by introducing technical and scientific terms, generally of western origin. The semantic value of the loans is respected and only a phonetic adaptation, in that case, is effected.

102

Much of the vocabulary of the sciences, of course, never moves outside the narrow specialist sphere and few of the learned borrowings have entered the core-vocabulary but some scientific words gain a more general currency, like *molekula*, *metabolizam, izotop, sonar, gên*. Words will move into general use if they bear closely on everyday problems of health and the treatment of disease (*vitamin, penicilin, antibiotik*), or if they are connected with widely used products of technology (*najlon, tranzistor, televizija*).

For the Modern Croatian period a distinction must be made between the adoptions from living languages and the formations derived from the two classical languages, or rather created out of Latin and Greek elements, and which might be called Europeanisms or even 'mundisms'. Although the Latin- and Greek-derived words, such as *antibiotik, astronaut, audio-vizuelan, hipotermija, izotop, kromosom,* etc. are strictly learned or technical, they do not seem foreign to the same extent as the recent loanwords from living languages such as *montaža, sputnik, kibuc, aparthajd, erzac, marijuana, skampi,* etc.

As modern civilization penetrates into the countryside, popular speech (vernacular) undergoes in its turn an important movement of vocabulary: concepts and words concerning traditional life are certainly going to be eliminated; new ones will be integrated. Popular language finds itself, at present, at the same cross-roads as literary language in the first half of the nineteenth century.[97] Inside Croatia, for example, the old rural dialects have been dying out, as a concequence of improved communications, greater mobility of population, the establishment of universal education, and more recently the rise of mass media. At the same time the urban dialect of the capital city, Zagreb, with its kajkavic substratum, has been playing the main part in the development of the Croatian language, as the American Slavist Thomas Magner clearly pointed out in his article *Budućnost je hrvatskog jezika u Zagrebu* (The Future of the Croatian Language Is To Be Found in Zagreb) in *Školski Vjesnik,* 1-2, Split, 1969.

Besides, lexical innovation and enrichment have, to a significant extent, consisted of a haphazard introduction of foreign loan-words by the media. Insufficient attention was paid to the internal rules of word formation in the language which would ensure that the enriched language would be easily understood by all speakers. In this respect the collection and sifting of genuine (native) creations for new concepts has been an important task. In fact many genuine creations had been in use but they were overshadowed by numerous loan-words. Klaić's Dictionary of Foreign Words and Expressions, Zagreb 1978, records about 45,000 items. These loand-words constitute, above all, international terminology of different spheres of human activity, above all those international neologisms of Graeco-Latin form which are common to all European languages and thus contribute to their covergence (cf. analogical creations *aerodrom, velodrom, motodrom, tankodrom* made on the pattern of *hipodrom,* or *kartoteka, filmoteka, diskoteka* made on *biblioteka*). The same can be said about the suffixes *-ade, -age, -ance, -ure, -ant (-ent), -ism, -ist, -ator, -ment,* etc. which constitute a great part of international derivatives. All these suffixes are to be found in Croat and serve to coin neologisms derived from foreign or even from native bases, e.g.

> *bakljada* 'torch-light procession'
> *drmator* 'influential Communist party leader
> *čehizam* 'Bohemianism'
> *zborist* 'chorister'
> *gnjavaža* 'nuisance'
> *prevarant* 'cheater'
> *uživancija* 'pursuit of pleasure'
> *vezist* 'an R/T operator in the army', etc.[98]

The impact of international technical and scientific terms, containing Greek affixes, on the vocabulary of all European languages, including Croatian, has been enormous. Such prefixes as *anti-* (against), *auto-* (self), *antropo-* (man), *filo-* (love), *fono-* (sound), *foto-* (light), *fizio-* (nature), *geo-* (earth), *hemi-* (half), *hetero-* (different), *hidro-* (water), *krono-* (time), *lito-* (stone), *mikro-* (small), *poli-* (much, many), *psiho-* (mind) and *tele-* (distance) each generate dozens of vital words in scientific, technical and other fields. Equally important suffixes of Greek origin are *-fon* (sound), *-fobia* (fear), *-graf* (write), *-gram* (letter), *-metar* (measure), and *-skop* (see).

By the end of the nineteenth century there was an attempt, in Croat, at replacing some foreign suffixes by native. Thus the infinitive suffix *-irati* of Franco-German origin was sometimes replaced by *-ovati*. Yet this attempt failed and the suffix *-irati* is used extensively in Croat to adapt foreign infinitives or to derive infinitives from foreign and even native bases, e.g. *urudžbirati* 'to enter in a ledger'. To this suffix corresponds in Serbian *-isati* which is also of foreign (Greek) origin, e.g.:

Cr. *grupirati* 'to group'	Sb. *grupisati*
Cr. *definirati* 'to define'	Sb. *definisati*
Cr. *informirati* 'to inform'	Sb. *informisati,* etc.[99]

One should also notice that in the enrichment of the Croat vocabulary the use of prefixes of foreign origin plays an important part; e.g. Greek *hiper-* and *hipo-*, *homo-* and *hetero-*; Latin *super-* and *sub-* (*sup-*), *anti-* (*kontra-*) and *pro-*, etc. These prefixes create a new grammatical category of comparison as well for the substantives and verbs as for the adjectives, e.g. *hipertrofija/hipotrofija, hipertrofiran/hipotrofiran, homogen/heterogen, superstrat/supstrat, antifašist/profašist,* etc. Thus the modern language has constituted a prefixal system of the notion of degree which essentially uses foreign prefixes: *infra-* (*infracrven* 'infrared', *infrazvučan* 'infrasonic') *ultra-* (*ultraljubičast* 'ultraviolet', *ultrazvučan* 'ultrasonic', etc.). The formation of the oppositional pairs (*hiper-/hipo-*, *ultra-/infra-*) allows to precise the nuances of the degree expressed by the prefixes and their formative disponibility tends to make of these prefixes true grammatical forms. Scientific and technical jargons have constituted a whole system of antonymous pairs borrowing from a Graeco-Latin model which has been adopted by nearly all European languages, namely *izo-/alo-* (*izomorfan/alomorfan*), *mikro-/makro-* (*mikrofilm/makrofilm*), *mono-/poli-* (*monosilabičan/*

polisilabičan), *neo-/paleo-* (*neolitik/paleolitik*), *mini-/maksi-* (*minimalan/maksimalan*), etc.

The suffixal elements of Greek origin which have a precise use [*-fil* (*-man*) and *-fob*] and serve to form substantives like *frankofil* (*frankoman/frankofob*), *anglofil* (*angloman/anglofob*) also belong to this grammatical category.

Of current usage in Croat are also hybrid words or compounds, based on a borrowing taken over from another language, in which one part is translated into Croat while the other is retained from the loan original though modified in form, e.g.:

polufinale 'a semi-final' (cf. calque *polusvijet—G.* *Halbwelt* Fr. *demi-monde*)	*naftovod* 'pipe-line'
nadrealizam 'surrealism'	*pod-sekretar* 'under- secretary'
protuakcija 'counteraction'	*reizbor* 're-election'
ne-oportun 'inoportune'	*neangažiran* Fr. non-engagé
beskompromisan 'uncom- promising'	'uncommitted'
	roman-rijeka Fr. roman- fleuve
besklasan 'classless'	

traperice 'blue-jeans'(in Serbian *farmerke, farmerice*)[100]

The dimension stretching from the unmarked core-vocabulary, which of course includes fully-assimilated loan-words, towards totally foreign words is particularly interesting. The borrowing of a foreign word is a gradual process. At one extreme we have fully-assimilated loan-words like *papir* 'paper', *vagon* 'railway coach', *kino* 'cinema', *teka* 'exercise book', at the other the quotation of totally foreign words or phrases in Croatian sentences: *cum grano salis, au courant, play-back, Weltanschauung*, etc. In the gradual transformation of a quotation or foreignism into a loan-word three steps of change can often be observed. First, the phonology of the word is gradually adapted to conform to Croatian patterns.[101] *Bulletin*, a 19th century borrowing from French, has become *bilten* with assimilation of the *u* and the nasalized final vowel to the nearest appropriate native pattern. The second type of change which affects loan-words is that, as they become more closely assimilated into the borrowing language, they become capable of producing derivative formations: from *kuraža* (courage) has developed adjective *kuražan*, verb *okuražiti*, etc.[102] Thirdly, loan-words often undergo a marked change of meaning as they become assimilated into the borrowing language: *perron* means 'flight of steps before a house' in French but 'railway platform' in Croatian (*peron*).

It is difficult to tell what will be the incidence of these neologisms on the Croat morphology and syntax.[103] In any case, the massive adoption of foreign terms poses to the Croat language particular problems. The penetration of foreign learned words into the Croat traditional vocabulary does not only bring about a transformation of the vocabulary but also jostles the autonomous rules of the language. The increase of loan-words and their penetration into general usage via mass media, in a society which is more and more dominated and conditioned by audiovisual contrivances, has for consequence the popularization of morphological and syntactical processes peculiar to loan-words and their use in colloquial language (cf. *prevarant/prevarancija*). Furthermore, a great number of borrowings with identical affixes create for speakers associative fields which end by becoming indispensable and characteristic of a learned, scientific or even colloquial language.

Between the two World Wars the German and French influences in Yugoslavia were very strong, due primarily to the numerous trade and political connections. Both French and German were taught extensively and on most educational levels, and their contribution to the Croat lexicon has been particularly heavy, both in terms of direct loans and of loan-translations. But whereas German loan-words have all been directly borrowed into Croatian, many French loans have reached Croat indirectly, through German and Italian. An example of the intricacies of indirect adoptions is provided by *bagaža*, borrowed in the 19th century from German (*die*) *Bagage*, itself an earlier adoption from French *le bagage*.[104]

A number of words were taken over from Russian before the October Revolution that have also entered the general international vocabulary, e.g. *nihilizam, nihilist, pogrom, kulak, boljševik, sovjet* etc. After the revolution many new words appeared in Russian, which refer to phenomena and concepts relating to Soviet reality as well as to innovations made or introduced in the Soviet Union. They may be designated as 'Sovietisms'. Many of them entered the international vocabulary such as *kolhoz, kominterna, stahanovac, kolektivizacija, traktorist* 'tractor operator', *udarnik* 'front ranker, shock-worker', *pjatiljetka (petoljetka)* 'five-year plan', *prezidium, sputnik, lunik, lunohod* 'moon-car'.

After the Second World War Russian loans left their stamp both on Croat lexicon and word-formation. The political jargon of the Communist Party has been instrumental in transferring Russianisms, e.g. *komesar* 'commissar', *pionir* 'a member of Young Pioneers (9-14)', *kolektiv* 'collective', *crveni kutić* 'Red corner' = the local Party propaganda room', *dom kulture* 'local community centre', *čistka* 'a Party purge', *aparatčik* 'apparatchik', *kult ličnosti* 'personality cult', *samokritika* 'self-criticism', *karakteristika* 'a character reference', *masovan* 'massive', *rukovodstvo* 'leadership', *rukovoditi* 'to lead'. It was probably under the influence of Russian that some *nomina agentis* (agent-nouns) were formed in Croat with the pan-Slavic suffix *-telj*, (*pokazatelj, izumitelj, prekršitelj, pazitelj*, etc.). This suffix has been recently challenged in Croat by suffix *-lac*; thus the Russian loan *rukovoditelj* has been changed into *rukovodilac* 'leader', although *-telj* is still very productive, e.g. *ravnatelj, upravitelj, čitatelj*, etc. Moreover, masculine nouns ending in *-lac* often cannot derive their feminine counterpart in *-lica* which clashes with the suffix *-lica*, used to derive nouns designating objects or instruments; thus *slušalac* 'listener' has no feminine counterpart since *slušalica* is 'a telephone receiver'. Hence the advantage of deriving the nouns in *-telj*, in order to avoid homonymic collision, e.g. *slušatelj—slušateljica, buditelj—buditeljica*, etc. (*budilica* 'alarm-clock', in Serbian *budilnik*). Many acronyms and telescoped words have also been formed on Russian models (cf. Russian G.P.U., N.K.V.D., K.G.B., *kolkhoz, komsomol,* etc.).[105]

Blending and acronymic formation are two minor   processes of word-formation which arise more from the fancy of an individual than the structure of the language. One can distinguish acronyms formed from the initial letters of other words, such as *KP* (from *Komunistička Partija*), *SKOJ* (from *Savez Komunističke Omladine Jugoslavije*), *OUR* (*Organizacija Udruženog Rada*); syllabic acronyms, such as *Na-Ma* (from *Narodni Magazin*), *Gra-Ma* (from *Gradski Magazin*) and telescoped words or blends *Jugopetrol, Jugošped, Jugomont,* etc. The development of acronyms and blends is a recent phenomenon in Croatian; no certain example of either is known before the 20th century. This process of word formation is very productive but words thus formed are not transparent. Thus the French calque *Papenov lonac < marmite de Papine* 'pressure cooker' has been replaced by a newly formed opaque acronym *pretis* (from *Pre*(duzeće) *Ti*(to) *S*(arajevo)). These acronyms are treated as lexemes and, if currently used, they are integrated into the system of the language as common nouns. They have grammatical gender, are inflected and serve as a base from which possessive adjectives can be derived by the addition of a suffix *-in, -ev, -ov;* e.g. *Namin izlog* 'a Nama shopwindow'. This represents a great innovation if one takes into account that till the end of the nineteenth century possessive adjectives were derived only from proper nouns. Many of these acronyms and blends come from West European languages, *DDT, FIFA, radar, laser, tranzistor, eskalator* (cf. also infinitive *besežirati* 'to vaccinate with B.C.G.' formed from French conventional pronunciation of the acronym B.C.G. with addition of suffix *-irati*; whence the derivatives *besežiran* (past participle) and *besežiranje* (verbal noun)). Most of the new words formed in this way remain proper names (e.g. *Unesco, Nato,* etc).

The influence of English and American in Yugoslavia has been very marked over the past thirty years and many terms connected with modern science, technology, film industry, etc. for which there are no native equivalents have been taken over from English without any attempt at translating them, e.g. *teleprinter, deterdžent* (detergent), *flashback,* etc. The massive intake of English vocabulary after World War II was so great precisely because much of it had to do with the language of science and technology. The Croatian language and rapid technological change do not make particularly happy bedfellows. The layman seeking a simple explanation of, say, how a computer works, is often treated to a barrage of technical jargon from experts which only bewilders him further. Even engineers, it seems, do not always see eye to eye on meaning.

Foreign trade, sport, and all kinds of 'pop' music have also been responsible for the influx of English words into Croatian, the assimilation of which is partly regularized in Rudolf Filipović's monographs.[106]

For curiosity's sake let us notice that the philologist R. Vidović who carefully studied the penetration of foreign Western borrowings into the Croat daily newspapers in the last hundred years, reached some very revealing conclusions. He consigned the results of his research to his study: *Kako valja — Kako ne valja pisati*, (Matica Hrvatska — Zagreb, 1969) from which we draw the following data (pp. 16-17):

Year	1853	1882	1907	1932	1957
Percentage of Western borrowings in daily press	2.2%	3.8%	10.8%	13.5%	33%

Although the statistical methods and the technique of research used by Vidović lack precision and encounter the virtual impossibility of complete scrutiny of material available, nevertheless this quantitative approach reveals undoubted tendencies in the field of borrowing and comes to fairly reliable results.

One of the most important tasks for language treatment in Yugoslavia has been the monitoring of the adoption of foreign words and their integration into the existing language system. A fairly stable practice has been developed in this field.

Croats write foreign words in their original orthography if they come from languages which use Latin script. Therefore, in Croat the distinction between foreign(isms) and loan-words is rather clear. Serbs transcribe foreign words as they are pronounced and transliterate the original Latin writing into Serbian Cyrillic. Consequently in Serbian a clear line between foreign and loan-words cannot be drawn.

Croat continues to accept loan-words in considerable numbers. Its overloading with structurally alien elements from European languages which are at variance with the underlying rules of Croat has led to a weakening of these rules. In this respect Russian influence is especially insidious because, owing to the structural affinity of the Slavonic languages, words could be borrowed from Russian with little or no adaptation. This influence is discernible not only in lexicon but also in word-formation and syntax. As regards foreign loan-words, the golden rule should be Horace's *est modus in rebus*. If care is taken that the adopted loan-words do not violate the basic rules of Croat language structure, their presence can contribute to the functional expansion of the language and positively influence its structural growth.

During the first decades of the 20th century, at crucial junctures of the history of literary Croatian and literary Serbian, a key issue in the emergence of national languages has been the standardization of the city dialect of Zagreb and Belgrade since these cities have become political and cultural capitals establishing standards. Their urban dialects are radically different from the rural regional dialects of Herzegovina and Vojvodina.

To-day in Croatia, the basic dialogue or interplay is not between štokavic and kajkavic or čakavic as in the 19th century but between literary Croatian (*književno*) and non-literary or popular Croatian (*neknjiževno*), which to a varying degree lacks the status of standards. The linguists are nowadays involved with social rather than regional dialect and the standard is becoming socially rather than regionally based. In short, the standard is not based on any one region but on the literary language which developed in the 19th and the 20th centuries. Although there is a distinction between national or standard language and literary language, their mutual impact has also to be underlined. "One characteristic of a national language is its being by essence and by definition written—first of all and necessarily written, and spoken on the basis of the way it is written. It is essentially what is meant by the German term *Schriftsprache*."[106a]

It surely needs to be recognized that the literary language —the language as written down—has itself a powerful effect on spoken language. The literary tradition helps to shape and conserve the spoken syntax of educated people and has a strong if indirect influence on virtually every member of the community by creating a canon of acceptability, i.e. speech habits and set of forms which are socially, intellectually and educationally acceptable.

The shape of modern written standard Croatian has been determined not only by the literary writers, translators, journalists and the overlapping lexocographers and grammarians but also by the men with the power. And this fact is what makes the discussion of the standard language such a current and controversial subject in Yugoslavia to-day.

Language Policy and Language Planning in Yugoslavia with Special Reference to Croatian

Grammatici certant et adhuc sub iudice lis est.
Horace, *Ars poetica,* line 78

When in December 1918 the Kingdom of the Serbs, Croats and Slovenes was created, later in 1929 renamed the Kingdom of Yugoslavia, the government in Belgrade insisted on national and linguistic unity: one language, Serbo-Croatian-Slovenian; one nationality, Yugoslav; one state, Yugoslavia. The government completely disregarded Yugoslavia's linguistic diversity while Macedonian and Albanian were suppressed. Macedonia was designated 'Southern Serbia' and Macedonian regarded as a subdialect of Serbian. In the new, South-Slav state, Slavic nations came together which were akin in their languages but very different as far as their religion, tradition and the level of their socio-economic and cultural development were concerned. The three major national communities, Serbs, Croats and Slovenes were characterized by their distinctive cultural and literary tradition and they were expected to overlook the religious and historical differences which had lasted for a thousand years.

The history of the new state was marked chiefly by the efforts of the Serbs to establish a centralized Serb state and by the vigorous resistance of the Croats and Slovenes (Roman Catholics and much more westernized than the Serbs) to secure some type of autonomy. The Serbs were royalists to the core, supporting the Serbian royal dynasty of Karađorđević. They were also 'centralists', opposed to any form of federal principle of government. Their own strong national feelings blinded them to the strength of the nationalism of the other peoples. Their attitude to the nationalities within Yugoslavia could not be expected to reconcile the nationalities to the

113

centralist control of a parliament and government which was predominantly Serb.

The Serbians treated Croatia as part of Greater Serbia, ignoring the promised federal constitution, and thus converting Croatian feeling into open hostility. Croats began to feel that they had been better off under the Habsburgs. Croat opposition was led by Stephen Radić, leader of the Croatian Peasant Party, who wanted some sort of free union of all the Balkan Slavs. In 1928 he was shot dead in parliament by a Serbian member, and parliamentary government came to an end. At best some safety-valve in the form of a measure of cultural and local autonomy was at times provided (1939), but it rarely sufficed to contain aspirations for independence among Croats, propagated by a minority and, in the end, tacitly accepted by the majority.

After World War I, D. Boranić published his first edition of the Croatian Orthography, established by Ivan Broz in 1892, and called it *Orthography of the Croatian or Serbian Language* (Zagreb, 1921) but despite its title, it was used only among the Croatians. During the next thirty years (until 1951) Boranić published ten editions of his Orthography. The Serb A. Belić, published his first *Orthography* for the Serbs in Belgrade in 1923. He too had a series of editions: 1923, 1930, 1934, 1950/52. Both Boranić and Belić followed V.S. Karadžić's principle of a phonemic orthography but their application differed in several respects. Maretić's school grammar of Croatian language was replaced in 1929 by Stjepan Musulin's *Gramatika hrvatskoga ili srpskoga jezika* (Grammar of Croatian or Serbian Language), an integrated grammar which by 1938 had gone through three editions.

On 6 January 1929 King Alexander, who already controlled the army, suppressed the Yugoslav constitution and took power. He resorted to direct personal rule to prevent the state from falling apart amidst the dissension. He abolished the historical provinces and divided the country into nine provinces (*banovine*) named after the main rivers, irrespectively of historical, national and ethnic traditions. At that time the name "Yugoslavia" was also officially adopted. The Croat and other parties were dissolved. The King was also head of the Serbian Orthodox Church which had a special position as the established Church of the old Serbian kingdom. Its power was demonstrated during the Concordat crisis of 1937. To the principle *cuius regio eius religio* was added a new one *cuius regio eius lingua* as the Serbian language became the official State language.

The American historian Ivo Banac succintly summarized the linguistic situation in Yugoslavia at that time by writing: "... Serbian ekavian was pushed through as Yugoslavia's official language, most often in Cyrillic garb. Nor could it have been otherwise. There was nothing neutral in the acceptance of ekavian, which was frequently the code word for the wholesale adoption of Serb linguistic practices, including the Serb lexical wealth. In short, Belgrade political centralism had a parallel linguistic direction, which amonuted to the infiltration of Serbian terms and forms throughout Yugoslavia by means of the military, civil administration, and schools." (*The National Question in Yugoslavia,* Cornell University Press, Itaca and London, 1984, 212-213).

A sham parliamentary constitution was established in 1931; and it became a little more real when the King was assassinated in 1934 and his cousin Prince Paul became regent. During King Alexander's and subesequently General Živković's and M. Stojadinović's dictatorships, i.e. during the decade 1929-1939, Boranić's Orthography was re-edited under the pressure of Belić's interpretation. Again, Serbo-Croatian linguistic unity was stressed as the main support for political unity. In the area of language, the government decreed that henceforth Belić's Orthography would be used in all public State schools. Far from fostering any unity this measure alienated the Croatians.

After the creation of the common state and the consequent influx of Serbian officials and administrators (and, after 1930, even school teachers) into Croatia, Serbian words poured into the Croat vocabulary. Even the phonology and orthography of Croat came to be affected by Serbian. The influence of Serbian on the Croat vocabulary began to threaten the individ-

115

uality of the Croat language and the purist reaction did not fail to manifest itself: first in the Zagreb daily *Hrvatski Dnevnik*, then in the philological periodical *Hrvatski Jezik* (1938-1939, No. 1-10) edited by S. Ivšić and finally in the publications of the cultural association *Matica hrvatska*. Thus Croat and Slovene purisms have expressed themselves in the struggle against the lexical influence of the Serbian language, especially after 1929 when the tendencies to create a common language for Serbs, Croats and Slovenes appeared and when Serbian acquired the status of a state language.

In 1939, Serbo-Croat political agreement (*Sporazum*) was reached on the autonomy of the Croat nation in Ban (Viceroy)-ruled Croatia, which was intended as the first step in the federal organization of the entire state. The so-called *Sporazum* (agreement) of August 1939 was concluded between Yugoslav Prime Minister Dragiša Cvetković and the leader of the Croatian Peasant Party Vladko Maček. On 26 August 1939, democratic government was re-established in Yugoslavia and new elections by secret ballot arranged for. The state was to be reorganized on a federal basis, the Croats receiving complete autonomy in all cultural and economic matters. The granting of extensive autonomy to Croatia on the eve of World War II came, however, too late and satisfied no-one. The military collapse and disintegration, both moral and political, of the Kingdom of Yugoslavia in just a few days (in the April War of 1941) were the result of internal confusion. The Kingdom of Yugoslavia was a pseudo-national state in which national amalgam had not held: Slovenes, Croats and Serbs are separate peoples. By 1940, following the Serbo-Croat agreement, Broz-Boranić's orthography was restored to its former position.

After the disintegration of Yugoslavia (April 1941) and after a new government was installed in Croatia under Italo-German protection, the linguistic norms were once again changed. In the interval (1941-1945) two editions of Croatian Orthography were published, one called *Etymological Writing* (1942) and the other *Croatian Orthography* (1944). The first was compiled by A.B. Klaić and the second by F. Cipra and A.B. Klaić.

116

In both, the phonemic spelling principle was dropped by introducing a new morphophonemic, 'etymological' erthography to be used as a norm of standard Croat, encouraged to be as distinct as possible from Serbian. This matter of orthographic norms changing with the changing of political regime is indicative of the close relationship between language and politics in Yugoslavia.

After World War II, Yugoslavia was again pieced together and a new authoritarian regime was imposed. The country was rebuilt on federal lines respecting ethnic, national and historical peculiarities. This changed the unitary Kingdom of Yugoslavia into a federation of six republics and two autonomous provinces. After 1945 Boranić published the last two editions (1947-1951) of his *Orthography* following Broz (1892-1928), not conceding to Belić (1929-1939).

One hundred years after the "Vienna Literary Agreement" of 1850 at which eight writers drew up a draft for the creation of a common Serbo-Croat language, the difference between Croatian and Serbian literary languages in the early fifties may be conveniently described as follows:

Croatian	Serbian
(a) Croatian literary tradition with Zagreb as its centre	(a) Serbian literary tradition with Belgrade as its centre
(b) Latin script	(b) Cyrillic script
(c) *što-ije* dialect	(c) *što-ē* dialect
(d) Boranić's orthography	(d) Belić's orthography
(e) Croatian technical and scientific terminology	(e) Serbian technical and scientific terminology
(f) Croatian abstract vocabulary for religious and philosophical concepts	(f) Serbian abstract vocabulary for religious and philosophical concepts

Post-war communist Yugoslavia was founded on the federalist concept of complete equality for all Yugoslav nations and nationalities, including the right to use their own languages. In Yugoslavia, the smaller national groups without a republic of their own are called the nationalities. Therefore in the 1946 Constitution there are four official national languages recognised, i.e. Serbian, Croatian, Slovenian and Macedonian. The guiding language policy of Yugoslavia, at that time, could be described as multilingualism which prescribes that all four official languages should be treated as equal. This was of course never the case in reality for although all nations and languages are equal, there are some nations and languages which are more equal than the others. But in the 1950's the idea of centralising Yugoslavia by "creating 'Yugoslavs' and a 'Yugoslav language' began to gain ground in top party circles in Belgrade and was reflected in the 1963 Constitution which reduced the status of the federal republics".[107] In this Constitution, and in all subsequent revisions of the Constitution including that of 1974, the "nations and nationalities are neither enumerated nor recognized as legal subjects. Articles 245-247 simply set forth the principle of equal rights for the nations and nationalities, including the right to use their various languages".[108] At the same time, due formal recognition was given to the national languages to neutralize language cleavages as a politically divisive issue.

In 1954 the Croatian Philological Society submitted to the Ministry of Education of the Republic of Croatia the manuscript of the new Croatian Orthography but the political authorities vetoed its printing. The most comprehensive dictionary of the literary Croat compiled by Julije Benešić met the same fate and has never been published.[109] Let us note that Benešić's Croatian-Polish Dictionary (*Hrvatsko-Poljski Rječnik*, Zagreb, 1949, 1304 p.) has 66,170 Croatian entries, i.e. more than Broz-Iveković's monolingual, all-Croatian Dictionary of 1901.

On 8th, 9th and 10th December 1954, twenty-five Serbian, Croatian and Montenegrin writers and linguists, drew up in Novi Sad, the capital of Vojvodina, ten points called the Novi Sad Resolutions. The participants urged a compromise between the Serbian and Croatian orthographies. A common Serbocroatian/Croatoserbian Orthography has been compiled by a committee of twelve members, implementing the Novi Sad

Resolutions based on the principles laid down in 1850 in Vienna. It is a well-known fact that the so-called Novi Sad Agreement was reached under political pressure and in an atmosphere of fear. (Cf. *Jezik*, XVIII, June 1971, p. 138).

Aa a consequence of the Novi Sad Agreement between Serbian, Croatian and Montenegrin linguists and writers in 1954, for the first time a joint Orthography was published in 1960, in Novi Sad, under the title *Orthography of the Serbocroatian Literary Language* and in Zagreb under the title of *Orthography of the Croatoserbian Literary Language*. Both contain the same orthographic rules (pp. 11-168) and spelling dictionary (pp. 177-882). There are four non-unified items: two scripts, Latin and Cyrillic; two sub-dialects, *ijekavski* and *ekavski*; many double forms are incorporated into the common Orthography so that one can choose between a Serbian and Croatian form; finally the spelling of foreign words.

Though this joint orthography did represent a "first" in the sense that the orthography of the Serbs and Croatians was compiled in a single book (two separate editions) it was primarily a *status quo* agreement. There was little synthesis, and a large amount of double listing, leaving it up to the user to determine which form he preferred. The whole problem of lexical differences in scientific terminology was left for some future date. This unified orthography contains both Croatian and Serbian variants and makes it possible for Serbian and Croatian speakers to use the variant of their choice.

"A frequent complaint against the joint *pravopis* (orthography) and the joint dictionary of *Matica hrvatska* and *Matica srpska* that resulted from 1954 Novi Sad Agreement was precisely that they failed to specify sufficiently what is acceptable in which variant."[110]

"Thus the Novi Sad Resolutions achieved the desired political effect of unity and left individuals free to use the variant of their choice. But who in reality enjoyed genuine freedom of choice? . . . Since the capital of the Yugoslav Federation was at the same time the capital of the Republic of Serbia, the Serbian variant of the language was used in the federal administration apparatus and in mass communications. Thus Croats

119

had to read or listen to it in the federal press, the dispatches of the official news agency, *Tanjug*, the nationwide radio and T.V. broadcasts, the post office, telegraph and telephone service, railroads, federal political and economic publications, newsreels, various administrative forms, the armed forces, diplomacy and central Party organisations. This practice continued from 1945 until the meeting in ,Novi Sad (1954) and up to the publication of the unified orthography (1960) and after. As a result, the Croatians felt that their language was degraded to the status of a local dialect, while the Serbian standard language became a sort of 'State language'.''[111] Thus the pre-war pattern of language policy in Yugoslavia repeated itself: the Serbian Standard has become superordinate, raised above other 'subordinate varieties'.

The Communist leaders in Belgrade believed that the changes of peoples' national consciousness would result from the harmonisation of socio-economic structures or levels of development. In spite of the intensive indoctrination through schools and mass-media as a means of the re-education process, the change of the different national and ethnical consciousnesses into the Yugoslav nation did not occur.

When the powerful head of the Secret Police, Alexander Ranković, was overthrown in 1966, the widespread dissatisfaction in Croatia with various aspects of Belgrade's nationality policy, including that in the field of language, came to the surface.

Even before the fall of Ranković, in 1965, the Slovenian Intelligentsia (*Kulturni radnici*) issued the *Declaration* regarding the use of the Serbian language on the Slovenian Television and in the Slovenian mass media. The imposed and natural penetration of the Serbian language into the Slovenian vocabulary had the consequence that in 1979 Slovenia's Language Arbitration Tribunal (*Jezikovno razsodišče*) was set up in Ljubljana, Slovenia's capital, to stop the influx of Serbian words into Slovenian when concern about the fate of the Slovenian language was first debated in public.[112]

A collective Croatian reaction against such *de facto* Serbian imposition came on 15th March 1967. On that day, nineteen

Croatian scholarly institutions and cultural organisations dealing with language and literature, represented by 140 signatories, including foremost Croatian writers and linguists, issued the "Declaration Concerning the Name and the Status of the Croatian Literary Language". In the Declaration, they ask for amendment to the Constitution expressing two claims: (1) the equality not of three but of four literary languages, Slovenian, Croatian, Serbian and Macedonian, and consequently the publication of all federal laws and other federal acts in four instead of three languages; and (2) the use of the Croatian standard language in schools and all mass communication media pertaining to the Republic of Croatia. The Declaration accused the Federal authorities of imposing Serbian as the official State language and relegating Croatian to the level of a local dialect.[113]

However, in Croatia today, there is no official orthography or dictionary of modern Croatian usage; the Novi Sad Agreement and orthography were rejected (1967-1971) and the Croatian Orthography (1971) was destroyed at the beginning of 1972, on the orders of the officials who had replaced the former liberal Croat Communist leadership (1969-1971). Meanwhile in Sarajevo (Bosnia) in 1972, there appeared for the first time in the history of the Republic of Bosnia-Herzegovina, the *Orthographic Manual of the Serbocroatian-Croatoserbian Language*, which is neither Serbian nor Croatian, and while not attempting to create a new standard, nevertheless claims to have one. As a result of politically motivated tergiversations and repressions by State authorities in pre-war and post-war Yugoslavia, Croats and Serbs are the only two European nations without a comprehensive descriptive grammar, an historic grammar, a standard dictionary of contemporary usage, a dictionary of rhymes, etc.

In 1967, as a consequence of the Novi Sad Agreement, the first two volumes of the *Dictionary of the Croatoserbian/Serbocroatian Literary Language*, were edited, published simultaneously in Zagreb by *Matica hrvatska* in Latin script and Ijekavian subdialect, and in Novi Sad, by *Matica srpska* in Cyrillic script and Ekavian subdialect. In January 1971

Matica hrvatska definitively rejected collaboration with *Matica srpska* on the "common dictionary" and on 16th April 1971 it renounced the Novi Sad Agreement completely, while *Matica srpska* completed its edition of the six volume Serbocroatian Dictionary in 1976. The condemnation of the Novi Sad Agreement by writers from Bosnia-Herzegovina appeared in the Sarajevo periodical *Život* (No. 11/12) in 1970. On 7th February 1971, the Association of the Writers of Montenegro also repudiated the Novi Sad Agreement which was consequently made void. [114]

Croat demands for greater economic and political autonomy led to mass demonstration in 1971 when the so-called "Croatian Spring" of 1968-1971 reached its climax. That same year political liberalization was abruptly interrupted by President Tito's crack-down in December 1971. Many Croatian political leaders resigned or were removed from office about this time. At the same time the Serbian minority living in Croatia was accorded preferential treatment and "it is probably no exaggeration to say that after 1945 and again after 1971, the Serbs behaved like conquerors". [115] In 1972 a widespread purge of Party and government officials started in Croatia, while leading Croatian intellectuals were jailed and put on trial. In the same year one of the most venerable Croat cultural institutions *Matica hrvatska*, founded in Zagreb in 1842, together with sixty of its branches throughout the country, was closed down. As a consequence, thirteen literary periodicals sponsored by *Matica hrvatska* ceased publication. Matica hrvatska's weekly newspaper *Hrvatski Tjednik* attained a circulation of 100,000 copies before ceasing publication in December 1971.

A century ago, a similar event took place in Slovakia. After the Austro-Hungarian 'Compromise' (*Ausgleich*) in 1867, the Hungarian authorities made great efforts to assimilate Slovaks by turning them into Magyars. They closed the Slovak cultural institution *Matica Slovenská* which was intended to be a central organisation for culture, science and popular education. In general, the status of the Slovak nation and Slovak language in the first Czechoslovak Republic (1918-1939) and during the first two decades of the Second Czechoslovak Republic (1945 up to 1969) was very similar to the position of the Croatian nation and its language in Yugoslavia. "The reconstituted second Czechoslovak Republic, or rather its political contingent, recognized in the so-called Košice government programme (1945) the existence of the Slovak nation with its own language; i.e. the *status quo*. This programme stipulated a symmetrical political structure for Czechoslovakia, with Czech and Slovak legislative and governmental organs. However it was in reality fulfilled only by the federalization of Czechoslovakia, the only lasting result of the Prague Spring of 1968." [116]

"As far as the Republic of Croatia is concerned, Tito's crackdown in the early 1970's left it in an unsatisfactory state, indicative of Communist inability to cope with the phenomenon of nation." [117]

Meanwhile, in Yugoslavia today the Croatian literary language is the official language in the Federal Republic of Croatia. This is expressly laid down in Articles 138 and 293 of the Constitution of this Republic (1974); but the status of the Croatian literary language within the Yugoslav Federation as a whole has not yet been clearly defined in the Federal Constitution of Yugoslavia, although in Article 269 of the Federal Constitution of Yugoslavia (1974) it is stated that the federal laws and the other general decrees of the organs of the Yugoslav Federation are promulgated "in the languages of the nations recognised by the Constitutions of federated Republics". This acknowledgement of the status of the Croatian language as one of the four 'official' languages of the Yugoslav Federation is only implicit. Art. 246 of the Federal Constitution lays down that "The languages of the nations and nationalities and their alphabets shall be equal throughout the territory of Yugoslavia" but it does not specify which languages. In practice Serbian serves as a *lingua franca* throughout the country. [118]

There is also the question, however, of to what extent the functional nondifferentiation of languages is carried out or thwarted in Yugoslavia. There are obvious limitations of

123

functional nondifferentiation of Serbian and other languages. In education, for example, in schools where Slovenian (Slovenia), Albanian (Kosovo), Macedonian (Macedonia) and Hungarian (Vojvodina) are the media of instruction, Serbian is compulsory, but in schools where Serbian is the medium of instruction, these languages are simply not taught. Other limitations affect the functional distribution of Serbian and other languages; for instance, while speakers of Slovenian, Albanian, Macedonian and Hungarian learn Serbian, speakers of Serbian rarely learn other languages. "Eighteen thousand Macedonians, eight thousand Albanians and six thousand Slovenians live in Belgrade. But there is no school or department for the teaching of their mother tongues!" At the same time, one cannot find Slovenian, Macedonian and Albanian dictionaries and textbooks in Belgrade bookshops.[119]

It is interesting to note that, while drastically suppressing Croat attempts to affirm their national identity, from 1945 the League of Communists of Yugoslavia promoted nationalism in Yugoslav Macedonia.[120] "The newly created Macedonian nation with its ethnic consciousness has been favored: this new nation has been allowed to pursue irredentism abroad, in Bulgaria as well as in Greece."[121] Macedonian is closely related to Bulgarian and is considered by some, especially the Bulgarians, to be merely a dialect of that language. However, since the creation of the Macedonian Socialist Republic in Yugoslavia during World War II, political circumstances brought about in August 1944 the recognition by the Yugoslav authorities of a separate Macedonian official standard language, although the speakers of Bulgarian and Macedonian dialects would certainly be considered by linguists to constitute a single linguistic community. Thus H.G. Lunt writes: "That Macedonians should accept standard Bulgarian for their own use would demand far fewer concessions on their part than have been made by Bavarians and Hamburgers, by Neapolitans and Piedmontese, and even within Yugoslavia by natives of Niš in the Southeast (Serbia) and Senj in the Northwest (Croatia)."[122] Thus, a more or less preliterate Macedonian dialect was raised, for political reasons, to the status of standard language whereas Croatian, a full-fledged language, with five hundred years of literary tradition, is being reduced to the status of a dialectized language or as Heinz Kloss would call it *Scheindialektisierte Abstandsprache.*

"To this day, many expressions of national feeling that have long been a matter of course in the other republics of Yugoslavia are apparently taboo in Croatia."[123] The Croats were being denied positive outlets for their own national identity in a very nationalistic country like Yugoslavia. In the Yugoslav system, being a Croat—and asserting Croatianness—implicitly conflicts with being a loyal Yugoslav citizen. It is here that Croats feel at a disadvantage compared to other nations or ethnic groups.

If the Yugoslav state concedes certain rights to the Croats, it is with reluctance. Under the most favourable interpretation, it acts only for the sake of its own reputation, but most often under external pressures or to parry the obvious danger of secession. The present system of 'constitutional' protection of the Croatian literary language in Yugoslavia is reminiscent of religious guarantees which do not exclude the aggressive atheism of public authorities.

There are nevertheless many Croats who demand the recognition of the Croatian and Serbian literary languages by the Federal Constitution in conformity with the decisions of the Anti-fascist Council for the National Liberation of Yugoslavia instead of the ambiguous terms Serbo-Croat or Croato-Serb.[124] On 15th January 1944, during the Second World War, the Antifascist Council for the National Liberation of Yugoslavia decided by decree (No. 18) that: "All the decrees and edicts will be published in four languages:Serbian, Croatian, Slovenian and Macedonian". This decree was signed by the President of the Council, Dr. Ivo Ribar and the Secretary, Rodoljub Čolaković; ergo it was legally ratified and has never since been abrogated.

Although sufficiently distinct from Serbian to be regarded as a separate language, litterary Croatian has been considerably overshadowed by Serbian. Thus, during the partisan war in Yugoslavia, the well known Croat writer Vladimir Nazor, the then President of ZAVNOH (Antifascist Council for the National Liberation of Croatia) and, after World War II, the President of the Croatian Parliament (*Sabor*), several times protested strongly against the imposition of the Serbian language on the Croatian press. This is reported in Vladimir Dedijer's book *New Contributions for a Biography of Josip Broz Tito*, Rijeka 1982, pp. 842-3.

On 19th December 1944, Marshal Tito signed the ordinance that the "Official Gazette of the Democratic Republic of Yugoslavia will be printed in four languages: Serbian, Croatian, Slovenian and Macedonian" (published in the Official Gazette of 1st February 1945). During the proclamation of the Yugoslav Constitution on 31st January 1946 in the Federal Assembly in Belgrade the Articles of this Constitution were read in Serbian (1-43), Croatian (44-76), Slovenian (77-114) and Macedonian (115-139).[125] Unfortunately, this constitutional practice has been discontinued. Quite recently, however, a Croatian edition of the *Službeni List SFRJ* (Official Gazette) has started to appear but the hybrid language used in this edition leads to such confusion that, for instance, the Croatian version of the Penal Code, published in the Official Gazette No. 44/76 (1976), contains 141 language mistakes, amended in the Official Gazette of 25 November 1977 No. 56, pp. 1982-1986.[126] The immediate future may well see the solution of this very acute problem, which is closely bound up with national questions and the political situation in the country, each subordinate nation seeking to keep its own distinct identity.[127]

Thus, the problem becomes linguistico-political. Many developments in this sphere have to be viewed against the historical background, and the subject as a whole is in any case fraught with various social and political implications. In fact, there has been in Yugoslavia from 1918 until our own time a constant struggle between the Serbian centralists and the Croatian, Slovene, Moslem, Albanian, Macedonian, Montenegrin, Hungarian and other federalists and a standing conflict between pan-Serbism and the opposing forces. The interplay of linguistic and political factors in Yugoslavia is not sufficiently understood in much of the world. Similar to the situation in other multilingual States, the language problem has long been an explosive political issue in the short history of Yugoslavia.

To illustrate the interplay of linguistic and political factors in Yugoslavia one can point out the analogy, *si licet parva componere magnis*, between (the status of) Serbo-Croat in Yugoslavia and (that of) Hindustani before the partition of India in 1947. Just as the colloquial form of common Hindustani (Khari Boli—which has no one orthography) served as the *lingua franca* of much of India and as the basis of two literary languages: Hindi and Urdu, two literary languages, Croatian and Serbian, arose from two different varieties of Serbo-Croatian. Urdu is very similar to Hindi in its grammar and structure, but being spoken by the Mohammedan population (Moslems), it has been built up from the Arabic and Persian spoken by the early Moslem invaders and is written in the Perso-Arabic script. Hindi is usually written in Deva-nagari (Sanskrit characters) and derives most of its vocabulary from Sanskrit. Literary Urdu and literary Hindi have become very much more different from each other during the past century, so that they really deserve to be ranked as distinct languages. Nevertheless, a compromise between the two, understood by speakers of either, has always been used for everyday speech and this form of the language, known as Hindustani, has often been suggested by Indian political leaders as a common language for the whole of India. To the cultural specialization of the two languages (Urdu and Hindi) have been added national and political forces since the separation of Pakistan from India. After the partition of India, Hindi became the principal language of India and Urdu of West Pakistan and the older term Hindustani, embracing both languages, has fallen into general disuse.

In a multinational and multilingual State, economic and political centralism, with its 'cultural' corollary as a side effect, inevitably leads to a form of internal colonization. The centralist encroachment of political and attendant linguistic hegemony precipitates the decline of national languages.

127

In trying to create one nation through oppressive State action, the State apparatus becomes the real steamroller used for crushing national cultures.[128] The idea of national unification passes through linguistic unification which is here in germ. In order to forge national unity and assure its consolidation, it is necessary to obtain, even by force, linguistic unity. Decisions about a language policy are normally made by politicians, not by linguists; and for political reasons which may seem valid at one moment but may have lost much of their force a decade later. Consequently language policy and planning are ways to dominate a people. Conversely, they may also become a weapon in the struggle for ethnic, national or class liberation. Nowhere is the power of lingustic politics seen more dramatically than in Yugoslavia. If linguistics as an objective field of science has to bend to political realities, then politics is presented to the Yugoslav public in cut-and-dried fashion to make it seem immutable and scientific.

The linguistic convergence between the two languages has been encouraged and hastened for political reasons by the Belgrade Federal Government which has imposed as 'official language' the Serbian language already in use in the political, administrative and military spheres. Serbian has been used for political ends as a cohesive force within the 'nation-state' of Yugoslavia. For that matter the convergence between the two languages concerns not only the language but the organisation of the social structure in which Serbian is the dominant language and Croatian the dominated. Thus, the Croatian words *povijest* 'history', *zemljopis* 'geography', *tisuća* 'thousand', *siječanj* 'January', *veljača* 'February', *općina* 'commune', *nogomet* 'football', *zrak* 'air', *kruh* 'bread', *kotar* 'district', etc., have been proscribed and forbidden for administrative use in the territories of Bosnia-Herzegovina since the Second World War.[129] The attempt to create a uniform norm of usage, by suppressing Croatian words in favour of Serbian ones, has had an ideological (political) dimension in the building of the modern state of Yugoslavia.

Furthermore, in Bosnia-Herzegovina, the region where the *i-je* dialect is most widespread, between 1945 and 1965 the lexical stock has been officially Serbianized and the use of Croatian terms prohibited in the press, on radio and television, and in schools and administration. At the same time the spread of the Cyrillic alphabet in this Republic has been fostered by the authorities and officialdom. Thus the main Bosnian daily *Oslobođenje*, printed in Sarajevo after World War II in Latin script, began from 27th February 1978 to appear half in Latin and half in Cyrillic script. This Serbian superstratum has left profound traces in the administrative language of Bosnia-Herzegovina, where a new variety of Serbo-Croat has developed.[130]

"Linguistically the Croats (Catholics) and the Moslems use the *ijekavian* pronunciation, as well as most of other features that separate the Croatian standard from the Serbian. The vast majority of the Serbs (in Bosnia) also use the *ijekavian* pronunciation, but in all other respects they adhere to the Serbian standard."[131] In this respect it is interesting to note the remarks made by the Muslim writer from Bosnia Meša Selimović who after World War II settled in Belgrade, where he died in July 1982. As he located the action of his last, unfinished novel *Krug* ('The Circle') in Belgrade, he started to write it in *-e-* language (*ekavic*) and all the characters in the novel speak *e*-language. After a hundred pages Selimović gave up writing in *-e-*language and reversed to *-ije-* (*ijekavic*), jotting down the following remarks on the margin of his manuscript: "Until now I have thought that the action should be located in Belgrade; therefore all the characters speak *-e-* dialect. But everything bothered me, the sentence was stiff, everything seemed foreign to me. Therefore I decided to transfer the action to Sarajevo (capital of Bosnia) so that the language used could be *ijekavic*. This is really my language, although I recognize that *-e-* language is more economic and modern. Later as I did not want to lose the ambiance of a large city, I have left everything in Belgrade but all the characters speak *-ije-*dialect. This is my vernacular and I do not have to record phonographically what my characters say."[132] It is obvious that, even after living for many years in Belgrade, Selimović still felt that *-e-*language was foreign to him.

Given the complexity of population which exists in Bosnia-Herzegovina, no single solution should be expected to serve all needs.

After setting up Bosnia-Herzegovina (long disputed between Serbs and Croats for ethno-linguistic and historic reasons) as a separate republic after World War II, the Belgrade regime has catered for Bosnian Serbs at the expense of Bosnian Moslems and Catholics in spite of the fact that Bosnian Serbs constitute the minority (32% according to the 1981 Census) of the population in this Republic. A series of convergent social, economic and cultural events has led to the emergence of Bosnia-Herzegovina as a political entity, especially since 1967 when Bosnian Moslems were recognised as a separate nationality. This national emergence is accompanied by a desire for cultural and linguistic autonomy and identity, the adoption of a distinctive linguistic symbol of national identity vis-à-vis the outside world. Debate has recently been initiated, chiefly in the Sarajevo press, on the need for, and selection of, a linguistic symbol of distinctive Bosnian identity.[133] As Bosnia-Herzegovina enters the age of conscious language planning, the issues explored will be of great relevance to the general concerns of language planning and sociolinguistics in Yugoslavia. Consequently it is only as recently as 1973, that the linguistic policy in Bosnia-Herzegovina has slightly changed and many Croat words hitherto banned from public use have been readmitted, at least semi-officially. Thus the dual terminology (Serbian and Croat) has been accepted in schools, e.g. *bioskop - kino* 'cinema', *fabrika - tvornica* 'factory', *sprat - kat* 'floor, storey', *gas - plin* 'gas', *hljeb - kruh* 'bread', *pasulj - grah* 'beans', *krst - križ* 'cross', etc. It was also in 1973 that the Institute for Language and Literature was established in Sarajevo to research into the contemporary standard language in Bosnia-Herzegovina; to study the history of literary language in this land in the nineteenth and twentieth centuries and to investigate the local dialects—their synchronic description and relation to contemporary standard language.

The institution of an 'official State language' in a multi-national, socialist and federal State such as Yugoslavia is in flagrant contradiction of the very principles of Marxism-Leninism.[134] But cultural, national and social motives are intermingled, and these are opposed both to linguistic convergence and to cultural blockage, since cultural servitude is harder to bear and more humiliating than economic exploitation or political oppression.[135] The Croatian, Bosnian, Slovene, Albanian, Montenegrin, Macedonian and other Federalists have been fighting for a long time to establish their claims by legal methods: they want linguistic equality and they denounce the discriminatory treatment too often applied to the Republics by the Belgrade government and administration. They share the general Eastern European view that language and nationality are congruent.[136]

In general, the minority nations and ethnic groups in Yugoslavia (Croats, Bosnian Moslems, Slovenes, Albanians, Macedonians, Montenegrins, Hungarians, etc.) which, as a matter of fact, constitute the majority of the population of the country, find themselves in a position where social and economic promotion is blocked by the presence of the dominant group, Serbs, and the dominant language, Serbian, which is used in Central Federal Government and administration, the armed forces, diplomatic service, etc. In a totalitarian State like Yugoslavia, where government and army jobs are a chief source of social promotion, language differences seem to be politically divisive if social promotion is blocked by the existence of one preferred language among several.

However, it is clear that language is not the sole divisive element in Yugoslavia. The linkage of linguistic cleavage with differences in social status and preferential treatment by the Federal Government have been central to the conflict. In some areas such as Bosnia and Herzegovina, where religion tends to overlap with nationality, religious cleavage has taken precedence over linguistic boundaries and distinctiveness. Bosnian Moslems developed a strong attachment to their Islamic faith which their ancestors embraced during the subsequent four centuries of Ottoman rule in Bosnia. On the other hand, as the recent events in the Autonomous Province of Kosovo have clearly shown, no institution is more central to renascent Serbianism than Orthodox Christianity. Among the Serbian dissidents some were drawn toward the Orthodox Church as a vessel of Serbian culture, a link with their heritage. Throughout history, the Orthodox establishment has reinforced secular power by preaching submission to the State among its faithful and it does so now. Therefore, it seems that the League of Communists of Yugoslavia has tacitly acknowledged Orthodoxy as an essential ingredient in the peculiar mixture of loyalties that holds the Yugoslav State together, a vital element of Serbianness. Conversely, The Islamic Community and the Roman Catholic Church in Bosnia which have recently more vigorously asserted themselves have been subject to more repression. Sixty years ago Max Weber wrote: '' 'National' solidarity among men speaking the same language may be just as well rejected as accepted. Solidarity, instead, may be linked with differences in the other great 'culture value of the masses', namely, a religious creed, as in the case with the Serbs and Croats''.[137] Language conflicts in Yugoslavia consequently remain an actual problem, as in the former Austro-Hungarian Empire.

In present-day Yugoslavia no group is more vociferous in its language demands than the Croats. They cling more firmly than ever to their language, tradition and outlook on life and suspect that the Serbs—having forcibly ruled them since 1918, when union of the two ethnic groups was attempted with very little success—are trying to destroy their identity and cultural autonomy. Down the years, being barred from the main positions of economic, financial and political power (in the Federal Government), the Croats have been made to feel that they are second-class citizens. Their demands for closer participation in political affairs are often accompanied by demands for language reform or for the rewriting of the older, official code in their own literary idiom. Such demands often represent political and socio-economic threats to the established ruling class which controls the distribution of administrative posts.

Thus, language loyalty seems as important as religious loyalty; providing a basis of political cleavage in present-day Yugoslavia. Rulers who repress, distort or insult national consciousness thereby manufacture dangerous nationalism. Like General Franco in Spain, who declared open war on the Catalan language and on Catalan nationalism, Marshal Tito of Yugoslavia 'angrily warned' Croats and Serbs in March 1967 to stop stirring up linguistic disputes.[138] President Tito's choice of Priština (the capital of the Autonomous Province of Kosovo) for his condemnation of attempts to stir up national animosities was believed to be intended to give his comments on the linguistic controversy a wider application. Before the fall of Alexander Ranković in 1966 the Albanian community in this province had been persecuted by the Serbian police; Albanian representation in the local Government had since been greatly increased, and this in turn had given rise to a number of nationalist demonstrations by Serbs. The traditional hostility between the Kosovo Albanians and Serbs had been heightened in recent years by the severe economic difficulties experienced by the province. Severe civil disturbances occurred in 1981 giving rise to the declaration of a state of emergency in the province and to a series of measures against members of the predominant Albanian population. The 1981 census had shown that 77.5 per cent of the Kosovo population were ethnic Albanians while 13.2 per cent were Serbs. However relatively few of the security forces in Kosovo spoke the dominant Albanian language, Kosovo being constitutionally subordinate to the republic of Serbia.

There has been plenty of evidence that many political issues are still interpreted from a nationalistic point of view (not necessarily chauvinistic), and thus the linguistic quarrel is only one aspect of the present day rivalry between the Serbs and the Croatians. If the centrifugal forces operating in Yugoslavia are limited to linguistic considerations, there is still ample room for internal reorganization that would better accommodate the national sensitivities of both Croatians and Serbs. A common language does not seem to be absolutely necessary to a 'nation'. Multilingual states can exist and prosper: Switzerland is a good example.

Recent events, however, have clearly shown that the recognition of the Croatian literary language by the public authorities is merely fictitious. In September 1971, a manual of Croatian Orthography, designed for primary and secondary schools, was published in Zagreb. Compiled by three eminent linguists (S. Babić—B. Finka—M. Moguš), it codified the present norm of Croatian spelling and orthography: "In all ways, from a purely language point of view, *The Croatian Orthography* is probably the most authoritative guide to enlightened language practice in Croatia today." Forty thousand copies of this handbook awaiting distribution were seized and destroyed on the orders of the political authorities.[139] This autoda-fé throws a particular light on the 'cultural' policy of the Belgrade government. But one copy of the Croatian Orthography survived, was smuggled abroad and reprinted in London in 1972. The sixth edition of the *Survey of the Grammar of the Croatian Literary Language* (*Pregled gramatike hrvatskoga književnog jezika*), written by S. Težak and S. Babić and published in 1973 in Zagreb, met the same fate as the Orthography and was also reprinted in London in 1974.[140] Similarly the philological work *Croatian Literary Language Today* (*Hrvatski književni jezik danas*, Zagreb, 1971) by Lj. Jonke was withdrawn from sale and banned. A large number of newspapers, magazines and professional journals were also banned. Only in April 1979, official authorization was given for the publication of a new Croatian Grammar—*The Reference Grammar of the Croatian Literary Language* (*Priručna gramatika hrvatskoga književnog jezika*, 527 p.; published by Školska Knjiga, Zagreb) to be used as a textbook in secondary schools. This structural grammar designed for students and teachers of Croat, has been compiled by seven linguists, members of the Institute for Language of the Yugoslav Academy in Zagreb. But a month after its publication, a Communist Party spokesman severely criticised its contents and the Secretary of State for Education forbade its use as a textbook in secondary schools. Simultaneously, the members of the Institute for Language (*Zavod za jezik*) of the Yugoslav Academy have compiled a comprehensive, scholarly grammar of literary Croatian: M. Moguš wrote an extensive introduction to this grammar; D.

Brozović covered the phonetics/phonemics, prosody and morpho-phonemics; S. Pavešić and S. Težak treated the morphology; S. Babić dealt with word-formation; and R. Katičić tackled syntax. Although the work on this monumental grammar has been completed and the manuscript on 'the syntax', comprising 1200 typed pages, was expected to be printed and published by Školska Knjiga in 1979/80, the whole project seems to have been stopped by political authorities and 'the syntax' has never come out.[141] By the same token, under the pressure of political authorities, the publication of *Orthography of the Croatian Literary Language*, a spelling dictionary of 80,000 lexical items, compiled by Vladimir Anić and Josip Silić, which was due to appear in 1981 has been delayed and will probably never come out.[142]

In 1978, Dalibor Brozović wrote the first short history of the Croatian language: *The Croatian language, its place within the South Slavic and other Slavic languages, its historical changes as the language of Croatian literature.* Brozović's treatise of seventy-one pages appeared as the leading article in a quarto volume of 750 pages, entitled *Hrvatska književnost u evropskom kontekstu* (*Croatian Literature within the European Context*). The book was published in 1978 by Zagreb University Press 'Liber' and contains thirty articles dealing with the history of Croatian literature. Immediately after its publication, a few contributions to this work were severely criticized and attacked on Radio, TV, a special symposium, and in the Zagreb and Belgrade press.[143] The main target of this politically orientated criticism was Brozović's treatise on Croatian language. When the expurgated English translation of this collective work appeared in 1981, under the title *Comparative Studies in Croatian Literature,* all the criticized articles, including Brozović's, eleven in all, were simply omitted.

No one should belittle the implication of these facts. This system of censorship suppresses the facts of life in many areas and cripples independent public discussion of almost any serious issue. Deliberate State intervention and interference with the natural course of linguistic evolution and changes will not facilitate multinational intercourse and co-operation within Yugoslavia. A language can become a focus of loyalty for a community that thinks itself suppressed, persecuted or subjected to discrimination. The Croats object to the authoritarian way in which the government enforces its edicts, legislating by decree and not allowing the regulations to be debated by the Croat National Assembly, The *Sabor*. They say that such sweeping powers over rights and liberties and such vaguely defined authority should not be conferred on the government. With respect to the language question, a truly open discussion (of the problem) would be more useful than an authoritatively imposed official solution to the problem. Instead of being co-official with Serbian and on equal official footing with other Yugoslav languages in the State legislature, government, mass media and army, the Croat language has been banned from these spheres of public activity, which obviously indicates that there is not the broad linguistic tolerance in Yugoslavia which should prevail in a democratic society. If, on the other hand, Croat is explicitly recognised by the Federal Constitution of Yugoslavia as a legitimate language and a vehicle of cultural identity, then the attitude of Croats toward the Federal Community will improve and equality of opportunity will be a more realistic goal in the country. In this respect the American Slavist Rasio Dunatov writes: "It would appear that denying the Croats their separate standard language has not contributed to the unity of Serbs and Croats, but has done it great harm. Good fences make good neighbours, and the strongest fence for an ethnic group is its language."[144]

Although Croatian and Serbian are, in varying degrees, intercomprehensible for many speakers, "mutual understanding cannot be used as a criterion of unilinguality, because it is no great problem for Danes and Norwegians, Czechs and Slovaks to converse, each man speaking his own language. Mutual understanding is a highly relative concept".[145] Behind this paradox lies the truth that an idiom superficially the same has its roots in each case in cultural patterns in many ways quite dissimilar, so that apparent ease of communication may remain a barrier to real understanding. Culture is the basis of social interaction, and language is the vehicle of culture. The French linguist J. Marouzeau has aptly summarized the question of language unity by writing: "The unity of language coresponds approximately to the unity of civilization." (J. Marouzeau, *La Linguistique*, Paris, 1950, p. 96). Walter von Wartburg writes in the same vein: "All those who speak a language partake of the same form of civilization; they have access to the same cultural goods. Language is even one of the means that allow a nation of high civilization to be aware of itself." (*Evolution et structure de la langue française*, 3rd ed., Bern, 1946, p. 4).

The decision to consider Croat and Serb as variants of a single language has been taken on political grounds since there is a general tendency to group European dialects within political frontiers as dialects of the national language of the country and to confuse a Nation with a State, since the frontiers of modern Nation-States of Europe tend to correspond more or less to language areas. As there is obvious overlap between the two, the permanent confusion between a Nation and a State has somewhat obscured the point at issue. As the Swiss writer Denis de Rougemont has put it, "The State is not the Nation, nor the Nation the State". The Croats' basic dilemma arises from rival, often mutually exclusive claims made upon their allegiances by Nation and State. Yugoslavia is not a multilingual nation but a multilingual and multinational State. Moreover, there is no standard Serbo-Croat nor common Serbo-Croat linguistic norm as there is standard English or standard French, that is to say a standard variety of the language used in print, which is usually taught in schools, spoken by educated people and used in broadcasts and other similar situations, i.e. the variety recognised as a model by the totality of speakers and which language model is accepted by a given community as authoritative. "On the other hand, the Croatian standard did unify and does now unify all Croats into a single speech community. This criterion perhaps more clearly than any other supports the autonomy of the Croatian standard."[146]

What differentiates standard language from dialect(s) is as much linguistic in nature as political. The distinction

137

between 'language' and 'dialect' is based very largely upon political or cultural considerations. Thus Mandarin, based on the pronunciation of Peking, and Cantonese, spoken in the provinces of Kwantung and Kwangsi, are treated as dialects of Chinese although they are more distinct from one another than, say, Bulgarian and Macedonian which are often described as different languages. Strictly speaking, both dialect and language are relative terms and it is difficult to use purely linguistic criteria to divide up varieties of language into distinct languages or dialects. It is because certain linguistic varieties were spoken by an ethnic group politically dominant, that this variety has become standard language. The administrative, economic and political centralisation of great European States has considerably modified the process of linguistic evolution in these countries. In the majority of European countries, there has emerged a State language which all the citizens were supposed to know. The French philosopher Roger Garaudy once said that: "a language is a dialect which possesses an army and a navy". When the political power is lacking, the national culture is reduced to folklore, the subordinate language withers away, crushed by a centralizing bureaucracy which administratively tends only to level down. The linguistic and cultural claim then becomes a popular component of a combat against bureaucratic and centralistic alienations.

In present-day Yugoslavia the two different standard varieties co-exist within the Serbo-Croat linguistic community. Children in Croatia are taught in the standard language of the country in which they live, i.e. in Croatian, just as children in Serbia are taught in Serbian. In the same way, Croatian writers write in literary Croat and Serbian writers in literary Serb. Consequently, the term Croatian literary language is fully justified. In fact, Croatian literature has undergone a specific evolution and, moreover, this language comprises phonetics, morphology and a lexicon which differ substantially from those of the Serbian literary language.[147]

While the language issue has long been an important element in the political history and social development of Yugoslavia (and certainly will remain so for a long time to come) there does not exist in Yugoslavia a permanent agency to deal with language problems at the Federal level. However, different processes of standardisation have been in use in Yugoslavia since 1945. Unification has been attempted under the influence of strong centralizing factors such as firmly established central government, army, mass media (radio, television, newspapers, magazines, spoken films, etc.) and has been brought about especially by central government policy in education. But centrifugal forces in Croatia, Bosnia-Herzegovina and Montenegro, such as national sentiment and spirit, a literary tradition, different regional languages (čakavic and kajkavic in Croatia) and, above all, the federal principle of government, have strongly opposed this unification. More-over, standard languages in Croatia and Serbia are based on different literary languages while in Bosnia-Herzegovina the standard language, based on neo-štokavic -*ije*- dialect with a mixed Serbo-Croat lexicon, is the consequence of a com-promise between Croat and Serb, constituting the bridge between the two linguistic communities. To-day in the Republic of Bosnia-Herzegovina, the Croatian and Serbian lexical differences are neutralized since both Croatian and Serbian terms or variants are commonly used. Thus, for instance, both Croatian *tvornica duhana* 'tobacco factory' and Serbian *fabrika duvana* are in common usage but the hybrid forms *tvornica duvana* or *fabrika duhana* are also to be found in the daily press in this Republic. However, there also exist in Bosnia-Herzegovina independent forms, typical of the usage in this Republic, which are used neither in Croatia nor in Serbia; e.g.

Bosnia	*narandža* 'orange'	*tukac* 'turkey'
Croatia	*naranča*	*puran*
Serbia	*pomorandža*	*ćuran*, etc.

Language policy in Yugoslavia consists of a series of alter-nations between centralist and pluralist tendencies. These tendencies are always present, only their relative emphases change. Language planning in Yugoslavia is an outgrowth from and instrument of political decision-making and overall social planning. The periodic expansion and contraction of centralizing political forces are reflected in periodic adjustments of language policy. Yugoslav language policy, therefore, has not been inconsistent although its alternations may give the appearance of inconsistency. Rather, the alternations have resulted from the basic contradiction, at least in the short term of pursuing simultaneously the centralist and pluralist goals of the 'two sides'. On the one hand Yugoslav policy seeks uniformity, centralization and affiliation to a 'civic' or supranational Yugoslav culture. This side is clearly associated with Serbian, which has been promoted by making it a compulsory subject in schools throughout Yugoslavia, fostering the influence of Serbian in Bosnia-Herzegovina and Croatia and by managing textbooks and mass media so as to favour Serbian. The major types of mass media attest to the unique and dominant position of the Serbian language.

The other side, in contrast, is committed to the development of ethnic cultures and to the use of national languages for social mobilization. It might be argued that social mobilization, even through the medium of national languages, leads ultimately to uniformity, centralization and knowledge of Serbian and that it is more expedient to exploit rather than frustrate sentimental attachment to native languages. Indeed, this has been one argument for their promotion, as in the case of Macedonian. Whatever the ultimate motivation, the deliberate promotion has unquestionably strengthened the national languages: Albanian in the Autonomous Province of Kosovo and Hungarian in Vojvodina. Although the forces facilitating the expansion of Serbian in Croatia and Bosnia were operating before the Second World War, the Government's careful promotion of Serbian has speeded its advance.

Since the formation of Yugoslavia as a state, every political régime wielding power there has had to deal with the language issue in one form or another. But none of them have thus far solved it. In present-day Yugoslavia, the Communist party policy of 'democratic centralism' is incompatible with the federal concept of State organization. Thus, whereas the League of Communists of Yugoslavia is organized on the principles of 'democratic centralism', the State is supposedly federated. This basic contradiction in the structure of government creates permanent conflict and impedes the functioning of the institutions. The present system in Yugoslavia has elements of federalism, mixed up in its communist dictatorship. For all its democratisation of the State structure, the League of Communists retains a monopolistic grip on the levers of power.

The recent events in Kosovo and elsewhere have clearly shown that Yugoslav communism is shaken by the nationalist heresy and is beginning to desintegrate under the impact of nationalism.

At a time when the structures of the Yugoslav State and the foundations of political and economic power are under challenge, the introduction of a genuine confederative system in constrast with a centralist system seems to be one of the basic conditions for the construction of a democratic society. But federalism will only be really complete with the termination of the policy of cultural centralism of which the Croats, like the Bosnian Moslems, the Slovenes, the Albanians, the Macedonians, the Montenegrins and the others are all victims, since all the Yugoslav Republics have a marked personality and have to defend a distinct linguistic and cultural heritage. A veritable mosaic of peoples, religions and languages, Yugoslavia offers many challenging problems and prospects to the language planner who must come to grips with such pluralism. The task, therefore, is to reconcile the national identity of each people and of each Republic with the development of the Federal Community, in other terms to reconcile nationalism with a supranational structure.

★

Notes and References

1 These dialects are named after the different forms of the interrogative pronoun *what?*, which is *kaj* in the *kaj* dialect, *ča* in the *ča* dialect and *što* in the *što* dialect. The *što* dialect, according to the reflex of the palaeo-Slavonic *jat* (*ě*), is divided into *i, e* and *je* speech forms, while *kaj* is mainly *e* and *ča i* where it is not *i-e*.

2 The oldest Slavonic alphabet known as Glagolitic goes back to the 9th century and was originally used for writing Old Church Slavonic. According to the overwhelming consensus of scholarly opinion, it is reputed to have been devised by 'Constantine the Philosopher' (St. Cyril, 827-869). It is sometimes argued that Glagolitic arose in the West as a highly stylised offshoot of Latin script. It was used by the Bulgarians concurrently with the Cyrillic alphabet and by the Croats on the Dalmatian coast, in Istria and in Bosnia. There are two varieties of this system of writing, the round one called Bulgarian and the square one called Croatian. "This alphabet was used in Great Moravia, and then in Bohemia and Croatia, Macedonia and partly in Bulgaria. Since the 12th century the Glagolitic alphabet has been limited to Croatia, except for isolated attempts of single Czech and Polish monasteries to borrow this Croatian habit in the 14-15th centuries. With the 16th century it began to disappear from secular Croatian writings and the area of its Church usage has become more and more limited but after the Second World War spadework has been undertaken among Slavic Benedictines for a new extension of the Slavonic liturgy. With these exceptions all the Catholic Slavs now use the Latin alphabet", R. Jacobson, *Slavic Languages,* A Condensed Survey, Columbia Slavic Studies, New York and London, 1966, p. 11.

3 For the evolution of Croatian Slavonic, cf. J. Hamm, *Hrvatski tip crkveno-slavenskog jezika* in *Slovo Staroslavenskog Instituta,* 13, 1963, p. 43-67; Vj. Štefanić, *Tisuću i sto godina od moravske misije*, ib. 5-42, and A. Nazor, *Jezični kriteriji pri određivanju donje granice crkvenoslavenskog jezika u hrvatsko-glagoljskim tekstovima*, ib. 68-86. D. Malić, *Jezik prve hrvatske pjesmarice* (Codex parisiensis) (The Language of the first Croatian hymn-book), Zagreb, 1972. For the literature in Croatian Slavonic cf. the material of S. Ivšić in M. Kombol's *Povijest hrvatske književnosti do narodnog preporoda* (History of Croatian Literature up to the National Renaissance), 1945, the first chapters. Cf. also Vj. Štefanić, *Hrvatska književnost srednjeg vijeka*, published by Matica Hrvatska—Zora, Zagreb, 1969, especially the introduction *Hrvatska pismenost i književnost srednjeg vijeka* (p. 3-62). E. Hercigonja, *Srednjovjekovna knji-*

143

ževnost, in the collection *Povijest Hrvatske Književnosti*, Zagreb, vol. 2, Liber—Mladost, 1976, appendixed by Bibliography of works on medieval literature, compiled by S. Damjanović. E. Hercigonja, *Nad iskonom hrvatske knjige*, Zagreb, Liber, 1983, 449 p. S. Gracciotti, *Il problema della lingua letteraria nell'antica letteratura croata*, in *Ricerche slavistiche*, Roma 15 (1967), 1-40. D. Malić, *Počeci hrvatskog književnog jezika*, *Prilozi za VII međunarodni kongres slavista u Warszawi*, Zagreb, Liber, 1973, 83-88. J. Tandarić, *Staroslavenski jezik hrvatskih glagoljaša*, *Prilozi za VIII međunarodni slavistički kongres*, Zagreb, 1978, p. 115-124. D. Fališevac, *Hrvatska srednjovjekovna proza*, Zagreb, HFD, 1980.

4   The oldest statute is that of Korčula, part of which already existed in 1214, but the most important for Croatian legal history is that of Vinodol, composed in the Croatian language in 1288. The Statute of Vinodol is a collection of legal rules compiled in 1288 in Vinodol. It is one of the oldest monuments of feudal law among the South Slavs and a valuable source for the social and economic history of Croatia. Written in the Glagolitic alphabet, it consists of 77 articles legally defining the relationships established in Vinodol after King Andrew II of Hungary granted that region to the princes of Krk in 1225. The Statute of Vinodol regulated private property, contracts, inheritance and other institutions of civil law. Primary attention was devoted to the judicial structure, legal procedure and penal law. The Statute of Vinodol remained in use until the end of the 18th century. There is also a French translation of this statute, published by J. Preux (*La loi du Vinodol traduite et annotée*) in *Nouvelle revue historique du droit français et étranger*, 1896. An English translation of the Statute of Vinodol by A. Ferguson appeared in *B.C. Review*, No. 14 (1978). Cf. Also J. Bratulić, *Istarski razvod kao spomenik srednjovjekovne Istre*, Zagreb, 1975.

5   Cf. P. Skok, in *Prilozi za književnost, jezik, istoriju i folklor* 18, fasc. 1-2 (1938), p. 292-301 (Beograd); F. Fancev in *Nastavni vjesnik* 48 and *Građa JAZ* 15 (1940), p. 182-200. On the "chanters" in the churches cf. K. Moskatelo in *Danica istarska*, 1952; cf. also Črnja-Mihovilović, *Korablja začinjavaca, Antologija čakavske poezije*, Rijeka, 1969; I. Pederin, *Pretvorba hrvatskoga iz crkvenog u književni jezik* in *Crkva u svijetu*, 1, Split (1970), p. 65-74; Id. *"Začinjavci", štioci i pregaoci*, Matica hrvatska, Zagreb, 1979, p. 19-116; J. Vončina, *Marulićevi "Začinjavci"* in *Jezičnopovijesne rasprave*, Liber, Zagreb, 1979, p. 71-105.

6   The Croat redaction (recension) of Mary's miracle plays appeared as early as the end of the 14th century. Beautiful collections of Mary's miracle plays are to be found in Ivančić's Glagolitic Codex (14/15 century), in Petris's Codex (1468) and, later, in the Collection of Glagolitic books printed in Senj between 1494 and 1508: *Mirakuli slavne deve Marie* (1507/1508) (Miracles of the Glorious Virgin Mary) translated from the redaction of the Italian collection *Miracoli della gloriosa Vergine Maria*, known as *Il Libro del Cavaliere*.

In 1507 *Naručnik Plebanušev*, the translation of *Manipulus Curatorum* by the Spaniard, Guido da Monte Rocherii, was printed in Senj; in 1508 were printed *Korizmenjak fratra Ruberta* . . . *protumačen z latinskoga jezika na hrvacki* (translated from Latin into Croat) which is a translation of Caracciolo's *Quadragesimale* and *Transit sv. Jerolima*, translated from Italian *Vita et Transitus s. Hieronymi*. Cf. I. Petrović, *Marijini mirakuli u hrvatskim glagoljskim zbirkama i njihovi evropski izvori* in *Radovi Staroslavenskog Instituta* 8. R. Auty, *Sixteenth-Century Croatian Glagolitic Books in the Bodleian Library*, Oxford Slavonic Papers 11 (1978), p. 132-135.

7 In his study *Srednjevjekovna jezična baština renesansnih hrvatskih pisaca* (The Medieval Linguistic Legacy of Croatian Renaissance Writers), in *Istra* Nos 1-2, Pula, 1978, p. 38-49, Josip Vončina states that research into the relation between the linguistic expression of the Croatian medieval and Humanistic-Renaissance literature is badly needed.

8 Cf. *Varia* (col. 32-65) in Matteo Bartoli, *Das Dalmatische*, t. II *Glossare und Texte, Grammatik und Lexicon* (464 columns), publications of *Kaiserliche Akademie d. Wissenschaften, Schriften der Balkankommission. Linguistische Abteilung* IV et V, Wien, 1906. Cf. also J. Fisher, *The Lexical Affiliations of Vegliote*, London 1976.

9 Cf. M. Moguš—J. Vončina, *Latinica u Hrvata*, in *Radovi Zavoda za Slavensku Filologiju*, Zagreb, 11 (1969), 61-81. The oldest Croat literature is polygraphic: ninety per cent of it is written in Glagolitic script, the other ten per cent in Croat or Western Cyrillic and in Latin alphabet. From the second part of the 13th century Croatia is politically and culturally more and more Western orientated which accounts for the spread of Latin alphabet and language, the recession of the Glagolitic and the appearance of *šćavet*. Originally the word *šćavet*, from Venitian-Italian *schiavetto*, referred to the church books written in Glagolitic, later it designated Čakavic popular vernacular of Glagolitic liturgy. The Croats in Bosnia and in Central Dalmatia also continued to use 'Croatian Cyrillic' (*Bosančica, Bukvica*). It is a cursive Old Slavonic Cyrillic influenced in its development and use by Glagolitic characters and Latin and Italian orthography. This system of writing goes back to the 12th century and was still in use at the beginning of the 19th century. In the Middle Ages it was used only by the Catholics and 'Bosnian Christians'; later, after the fall of Bosnia under the Turkish rule (1463) by Bosnian Moslems. As early as 1493 the Venitian printer Andrea Torresano d'Asola published a Croatian Breviary in the Cyrillic Script (*Breviarium Croaticum — Hunc breviarium impressit magister Andreas de thoresanis d'Asula die 13 marcij 1493* in -8° in two volumes. Since then a certain number of spiritual and edifying books have been printed in Bosančica. Among the oldest books printed in this script are a *Book of Hours* and *The Prayers of St. Brigitte in front of the Crucifix*. The only extant copies of these books, printed in 1512 in Venice, are to be found in the Bibliothèque Nationale in Paris. The luxurious

graphical presentation of these works in the style of French "Livres d'heures" of the same period is of particular note. In the 17th century among the books printed in the same Bosnian Cyrillic characters one should cite *Nauk Karstijanski* (a copy of which could be found in the Bodleian Library at Oxford) and *Beside svarhu Evangelija* by M. Divković (1563-1631) and other edifying works of Catholic monks S. Margitić, S. Matijević and S. Posilović published several times up until the first half of the 18th century. Cf. B. Zelić-Bučan, *Bosančica u srednjoj Dalmaciji*, in *Historijski Arhiv*, III, Split, 1961. Id., *Problematika srednjovjekovnih hrvatskih ćirilskih spomenika*, in *Marulić*, August 1975, 235-240; M. Dizdar, *Stari bosanski tekstovi*, Sarajevo, 1971. V. Grubišić, *Grafija Hrvatske Lapidarne Ćirilice*, München, 1978.

10   Cf. J. Hyrkkänen, *Der lexicalische Einfluss des Italienischen auf das Kroatische des 16. Jahrhunderts. Die italienischen Lehnwörter im Sprachgebrauch der dalmatischen Kroaten im Lichte der kroatischen Renaissance-Literatur*, Helsinki, 1973, 637 p.

11   Cf. J. Torbarina, *The Slav Petrarchists of Renaissance Dalmatia* in *Review of National Literatures*, 51 : 86-100.

12   Riccardo Picchio, *Guidelines for a Comparative Study of the Language Question among the Slavs*, Vol. I, p.41. Picchio's *Guidelines* introduce *Aspects of the Slavic Language Question*, 2. Vols., Yale Russian and East European Publications, No. 4 (New Haven, 1984). On the Croatian language question, see S. Graciotti, *Il problema della lingua letteraria croata e la polemica tra Karaman e Rosa*, Ricerche Slavistiche, 13 (1965), 120-162. Ivo Banac, *Main Trends in the Croat Language Question*, in Aspects of the Slavic Language Question, vol. I, 189-259; cf. also Michael B. Petrovich, *The Croatian Humanists: Cosmopolites or Patriots*, in Journal of Croatian Studies, 1979, 20:17-36.

13   For all the following on the Croatian literature of the previous centuries cf. M. Kombol, *op. cit. passim*, with the bibliography at the end of the book (also in the new edition of 1961); similarly, the article of Lj. Jonke, *Štokavski dijalekt u književnosti do XIX st.* in *Enciklopedija Jugoslavije*, Vol. IV, p. 520-521, a. 1960;cf. the articles of Mate Hraste *Čakavski književni jezik*, ib. p. 525-526, and *Kajkavski književni jezik*, p. 526-528. Kombol's work and the articles cited give the bibliography on this subject. Cf. also the history of Croatian and Serbian lexicography by V. Putanec in *Enciklopedija Jugoslavije*, Vol. V (1962), p. 503-511. D. Brozović, *O hrvatskom književnom jeziku 16 stoljeća*, in *Zbornik Zagrebačke Slavističke škole*, Zagreb (1973), p. 129-135; M. Moguš, *Stilistički elementi hrvatskog jezika 16 stoljeća*, in *Zbornik* (ibidem), 119-128. V. Grubišić, *La Syntaxe de la langue de Marko Marulić* (Doctoral thesis, Aix-en-Provence, 1972).

14 M. Tomasović, *Croatian Renaissance Literature in the European Context*, 95-123, in *Comparative Studies in Croatian Literature*, Zagreb, 1981.

15 Cf. C.A. Van den Berk, *Y a-t-il un substrat čakavien dans le dialecte de Dubronik?* Gravenhage, 1958. Cf. also J. Vončina, *Jezična starina u hrvatskom petrarkizmu*, in Prilozi za VIII Međunarodni slavistički kongres, Zagreb, 1978, p. 141-162.

16 R. Auty, *Literary Language and Literary Dialect in Medieval and Early Modern Slavonic Literatures* in *The Slavonic and East European Review*, Vol. 56 Number 2, April 1978, p. 192-201. Cf. A. Kadić, *The Croatian Renaissance* in *Slavic Review*, vol. XXI Number 1, March 1962, 65-88; M. Franičević, *Čakavski pjesnici Renesanse*, Zagreb 1974. Id. *Judita Pjesme*, Zagreb 1974. J. Vončina, *Analize Starih Hrvatskih Pisaca*, Čakavski Sabor, Split 1978. Cf. also *Hrvatska Književnost 17. stoljeća i njezin jezik* in *Zbornik Zagrebačke Slavističke škole* 2 (1974).

17 Cf. T. Maretić, *Istorija hrvatskog pravopisa latinskijem slovima*, Zagreb, 1889, p. 365.

18 F. Fancev, *Jezik hrvatskih protestantskih pisaca 16. vijeka* in *Rad JAZU*, knj. 212, Zagreb, 1916. F. Bučar, *Povijest hrvatske protestantske književnosti*, Zagreb, 1910.

19 For a brief historical survey of the name of the Croatian language through the centuries see I. Ostojić, *Kako su Hrvati nazivali svoj jezik*, in *Kolo* 1/2 (1971); B. Zelić-Bučan, *Narodni naziv hrvatskog jezika tijekom hrvatske povijesti*, in *Jezik* 1971/72, 1-18, 38-48.

20 For the origin and evolution of the *kaj* dialect, cf. S. Ivšić, *Jezik Hrvata kajkavaca* (The language of the *kaj* Croats) in *Ljetopis JAZU*, Knj. 48, pp. 47-88, Zagreb, 1936, and above all the dissertation of Z. Junković, *Jezik Antuna Vramca* (The language of A. Vramec) in *Rad Jugoslavenske Akademije*, Zagreb, No. 363 (1972).

21 Cf. C.A. Van den Berk, *Y a-t-il un substrat čakavien dans le dialecte de Dubronik?*, p. 15.

22 C.A. Van den Berk, ibidem, p. 23.

23 Cf. the review by B. Franolić in *Lingua*, Vol. 52 (1980), 369-373.

23a Cf. Micaela S. Iovine, *The "Illyrian Language" and the Language Question among the Southern Slavs in the Seventeenth and Eighteenth Centuries*, in Aspects of the Slavic Language Question, Vol. 1, 101-156. Yale, New Haven 1984.

147

24   Cf. James B. Bukowski, *The Catholic Church and Croatian National Identity: From the Counter-Reformation to the Early Nineteenth Century*, in *East European Quarterly* 1979, 13 (3) : 327-338.

25   The poetry of Kačić, inspired by the popular *što* songs, also recalls in its diction that of the *začinjavci*. Cf. I. Pederin, *Kačićeva književna terminoalogija i narodna pjesma*, in *Kritika* 10 (1970), 43-51.

26   Cf. J. Hamm, *Etymologicon Illyricum*, in *Nastavni vjesnik* No 1-2, Zagreb 1942-43. B. Vodnik, *Povijest književnosti hrvatske*, Zagreb 1913, 353-355.

27   "But elsewhere, other writers, closer to the people, set themselves the task of speaking to them in their own language. In Bosnia, where a very harsh agrarian system kept the Christians in poverty, the Catholic faith and national feeling had to be defended; in Slavonia, the population, which had not been completely liberated from the Turkish occupation until 1718, had to be re-educated. This was the work of the Franciscans and also of the Jesuits. They continued the tradition of the religious writers of Bosnia and Croatia in the seventeenth century, but a new spirit appeared. The Dalmatian Franciscan Kačić-Miošić in his 'Pleasant |Discourse of the Slav People' (1756) composed poems in the language and almost in the tone of the folk poetry and his book had a great success among the people themselves. [Kačić's work was translated into Serbian by Gavrilo Kovačević and published in Novi Sad in 1818.] In Slavonia, it was a layman, Reljković, a soldier of the Seven Years War, who devoted to the education of the people a work inspired by the moralising literature of the 'century of enlightenment' and of Josephinism: his 'Satyr' (1762) was read not only by Catholics, but was translated into Serbian (1793)" — A. Vaillant, *La formation de la langue littéraire serbo-croate, Revue des Etudes Slaves* XXVIII (1951), p. 81. At the beginning of the 19th century some other Croatian literary works appeared in Serbian: Vid Došen's *Seven Headed Dragon* was translated into Slaveno-Serbskij in 1803 by Georgije Mihaljević. In 1827 Jevta Popović adapted to Serbian language Gundulić's *Osman*. — Cf. also S. Babić, *Jezik starih hrvatskih pisaca u Slavoniji*, in *Godišnjak Ogranka Matice Hrvatske*, Vinkovci 1968, No. 6, 71-84. Cf. also D. Brozović, *Uloga bosanskohercegovačkih franjevaca u formiranju hrvatske književnosti i kulture, od Divkovića do Martića*, in *Godišnjak Instituta za izučavanje jugoslovenskih književnosti u Sarajevu* 2 (1973), 35-53. K. Georgijević, *Hrvatska književnost od 16 do 18 stoljeća u sjevernoj Hrvatskoj i Bosni*, Zagreb 1969, 158 pp.

28   Cf. D. Brozović, *O početku hrvatskoga jezičnog standarda*, in *Kritika* No. 10, Zagreb (1970), 21-42; Id. *Standardni jezik*, Zagreb, 1970, 127-158; Id. *Die Entwicklungsetappen bei der Bildung des Kroatischen neuštokavischen Sprachstandards 1750-1900. Die Welt der Slaven*, 1976, 21, n° 2, 14-27; Z. Vince, *Ein früher Vorschlag zur Normierung einer einheitlichen Literatur-*

sprache bei den Kroaten, Die Welt der Slaven, 1976, 21 n° 2, 173-179; Ch. Spalatin, *The Rise of the Croatian Standard Language* in *Journal of Croatian Studies,* Vol. 14 (1975), 3-18.

29   Stulli's influence on Croat lexicography and literature was decisive. He laid the groundwork on which the Dictionary of Yugoslav Academy (Zagreb 1881-1976) is based. Vladimir Mažuranić in his Contributions to Croatian Legal-Historical Dictionary (Zagreb, 1908-1923) refers to Stulli 900 times. P. Skok's *Etymological Dictionary* (Zagreb 1971-1974) refers to Stulli 1200 times and R. Simeon's *Encyclopedic Dictionary of Linguistic Terminology* (Zagreb, 1969) refers to Stulli 500 times. It is interesting to note that A. Jal's *Glossaire nautique — Répertoire polyglotte des termes de marine anciens et modernes* (Paris 1848-1850, 1591 p.) contains a few hundred Croatian nautical terms taken from Stulli's Dictionary.

30   Thus, the following grammars were printed in Venice: T. Babić, *Prima grammaticae institutio pro Tyronibus Illyricis accomodata,* 1712, 1745; L. Ljubušak-Šitović, *Grammatica latino-illyrica,* 1713, 1742, 1781. Later were printed: B. Tadijanović, *Svašta pomalo ili kratko složenje imena i riči u ilirski i njemački jezik,* Magdeburg, 1761; M. Relković, *Nova slavonska i nimačka gramatika,* Zagreb, 1767, 1774, 1789; M. Lanosović, *Neue Einleitung zur slavonischen Sprache,* Osijek, 1778, 1789, 1795; Sebastiano Dolci (Slade), *Dissertatio de Illyricae linguae vetustate et amplitudine,* Ancona, 1754, 1774; Joseph Giurina, *Grammatica illyrica* Venezia, 1793. Josip Jurina also compiled trilingual dictionaries; the most important is the huge *Calepinus trium linguarum* (in manuscript); cf. M. Kosor in Rad JAZU, knj. 303 and knj. 315. All these manuals are written in što-i dialect.

31   Cf. P. Skok, *La littérature croate sous Napoléon,* in AIFZ VIII (1944) No. 24-25, 71-83. Cf. also V. Anić, *Akcenat u gramatici Šime Starčevića,* in *Radovi filozofskog fakulteta u Zadru,* Zadar, 7 (4) (1968), 70-88. Z. Vince, *Zasluge Šime Starčevića za hrvatski književni jezik,* in *Filologija* 7 (1973), 157-201. Id. *Jezična pitanja u "Ilirskim Provincijama",* in *Putovima hrvatskog književnog jezika,* 114-131, Zagreb, 1978. Z. Junković, *Šime Starčević i fonološki opis novoštokavskih naglasaka,* in *Jezik* 25 (3), 80-85 (1977/78).

32   Between 1933 and 1975 sixteen anthologies of kajkavic poetry, comprising one hundred and nine poets, were edited in Croatia. (Cf. M. Kuzmanović, *Antologija Novije Kajkavske Lirike,* in *Kaj* 3-5, Zagreb 1975, 257-289). Many *kaj* and *ča* poetry and prose works remain masterpieces of Croatian literature, for instance Galović's *Z mojih bregov* (1913-1914), Krleža's *Balade Petrice Kerempuha* (*Les Ballades de Petritsa Kerempuh,* Paris, 1975, Collection UNESCO d'oeuvres représentatives), Goran Kovačić's *Ognji i Rože* (Fires and Roses) (1945); the *ča* stories, *Libar Marka Uvodića Splićanina,* etc. The most famous of modern Croat writers Miroslav Krleža has written about the peasant rebellion of Matija Gubec in 1573 and its aftermath in his *Ballads*

of Petrica Kerempuh, written in the kajkavic, almost macaronic, Zagreb seventeenth century dialect. *Ballads* have been translated into Serbian by Viško Raspor (cf. the Belgrade weekly *NIN*, 10. 1. 1982, p. 40-41, and 3. 1. 1982, p. 3, 6) — The monthly literary periodical *Kaj*, edited in Zagreb since 1958, is evidence of the kajkavic literary revival and of the excellence of the contributions which appear in its current issues. There are also to be found many first-class articles dealing with the linguistic aspects of *kaj* dialect. — Cf. also T.F. Magner, *A Zagreb Kajkavian Dialect*, Pennsylvania State University, 1966. — Since 1971 the periodical *Čakavska Rič (Čakavic Word)* has been published in Split, devoted to the čakavic dialect. — Cf. H. Steinhauer, *Čakavian Studies*, The Hague, Mouton, 1973. Cf. D. Brozović, *O Modernoj hrvatskoj dijalektalnoj poeziji*, in *Antologija novije hrvatske lirike*, Zagreb, Lykos, 1958, 9-22. Id. *O tronarječnoj dimenziji hrvatske književnosti*, in *Croatica*, 7-8 (1976), 11-18. P. Šegedin, *Pitanja hrvatskog književnog jezika*, in *Encyclopaedia Moderna*, No. 13, 1970, 58-63. M. Franičević, *Problem dijalekata u hrvatskoj književnosti*, in *Panorama hrvatske književnosti XX stoljeća* (Panorama of the 20th c. Croatian literature), Zagreb, 1965, 739-767. M. Moguš, *Čakavsko narječje (Fonologija)*, Školska knjiga, Zagreb, 1977. M. Hraste—P. Šimunović, *Čakavisch-deutsches Lexicon*, Köln, 1979. — Croat regional literature emphasizes the regional characteristics of *locale* or setting by stressing local speech. One cannot, however, accept the implication that the regional setting of a work written in a dialect somehow detracts from its validity. If 'regionalism' implies escapism, retreat from the problems of the time then the term is certainly inappropriate to describe contemporary čakavic or kajkavic poetry.

33   This continuity between the modern literary language and the ancient literary language has been clearly brought out by S. Ivšić, who writes that "the Croatian literary što language of today is merely an organic prolongation of our literary language which we had before Vuk, and Vuk, who is indeed the father of the Serbian literary language, clearly recognised it. . . " (cf. S. Ivšić, *Hrvatski književni jezik, in* Hrvatski jezik, No. 2-3, Zagreb, 1938, p. 35). Cf. also J. Vončina, *O kontinuitetu hrvatskoga književnog jezika od 15 do 18 stoljeća*, in *Priloži za VII međunarodni kongres slavista u Warszawi*, Zagreb, Liber, 1973, 165-177. R. Katičić, *Opseg povijesti hrvatskog jezika*, in *Hrvatski znanstveni zbornik* 1 (1971), 27-42. Z. Vince, *Od Baščanske ploče do Kačića i Reljkovića*, in *Putovima hrvatskoga književnog jezika*, 17-96, Zagreb, 1978. I. Pederin, *"Začinjavci", štioci i pregaoci*, Matica hrvatska, Zagreb, 1979.

34   R. Auty, *Pannonian Parallels and Divergences. Thoughts on the History of the Croatian and Hungarian Literary Languages*, in Filologija 8, 29-36 (1978).

35   R. Auty, ibid.

36   R. Katičić, *O početku novoštokavskoga hrvatskoga jezičnog standarda,*
. . . in Filologija (1978), p. 180.

37   In this respect M. Hraste, late Professor of Slavic Philology at Zagreb
University writes: "It is well known that the Serbian literary language has had
a completely different development from the Croatian literary language,
be it due to the determination of Serbian writers, or, for a certain time, to the
historical circumstances. From the first written monuments to the times of
Vuk Karadžić, the middle of the nineteenth century, the language of Serbian
literature has always been an artificial one (Serbian-Slavonic, Russian-
Slavonic, Slavonic-Serbian) and has had very little to do with the speech of
the Serbian peasant. That is why Vuk Karadžić fought so courageously and
uncompromisingly for the introduction into literature of the language of the
ignorant peasantry. That was not the case with Croatian literature. From the
very first days of written Croatian in the twelfth century (Baška Tablet) to the
Illyrian National Awakening in the nineteenth century, when the Croatians
started writing their literary works in the štokavian dialect exclusively, the
non-ecclesiastic (lay) Croatian literature was written in the vernacular and in
all three dialects (čakavic, kajkavic and štokavic), in most cases according to
the dialect spoken in the writer's province." (M. Hraste, *Strani elementi
u hrvatskom ili srpskom narodnom i književnom jeziku,* in *Radovi Slavenskog
Instituta u Zagrebu,* II (1958), 43. Cf. B. Ungegaun, *Les débuts de la langue
littéraire chez les Serbes,* Paris, 1935. Cf. also A. Albin, *The Creation of the
Slaveno-Serbski Literary Language,* in *The Slavonic and East European
Review,* London, 113 (Oct. 1970), 483-491.

38   For the history of the constitution of the modern literary language
among the Croats and the Serbs, see Ljudevit Jonke, *Die Entstehung der
neueren Schriftsprache bei den Kroaten und Serben im 19 Jahrhundert
(Aus der Geistwelt der Slawen),* in *Festschrift Erwin Koschmieder,*
1967, 55-67.

39   R. Auty, *The Role of Poetry in the early nineteenth-century Slavonic
language revivals,* in *Revue des Etudes Sud-Est Européennes,* tome XI
(1973) No. 1, p. 34.

40   R. Auty, *The Linguistic Revival Among the Slavs of the Austrian
Empire, 1780-1850: The Role of Individuals in the Codification and Acceptance of New Literary Languages,* in *The Modern Language Review,* Vol. 8
(1958), p. 400. Cf. also A. Barac, *Demetrove misli o književnom jeziku,* in
Hrvatski Jezik I (1938), 79-84.

41   On this subject, the Serbian philologist M. Stefanović writes: "and what
is still more important is the tradition, the long tradition of the existence of the
national literary language among the Croats which has naturally conditioned
another attitude towards the literary language of the past. This tradition,

however, did not exist at all among the Serbs, which explains the divergence of views as to the literary language between Vuk Karadžić and the Illyrians". (Cf. *Savremeni srpskohrvatski jezik*, Belgrade, 1964, p. 46). Cf. M. Moguš, *Odnos Iliraca prema kontinuitetu 'hrvatskoga književnog jezika*, in *Prilozi za VII Međunarodni Kongres Slavista u Warszawi*, Zagreb, Liber, 1973.

42   "The Serbs and the Croats lived separately up to the first World War, developing their cultural activity and their literature in parallel and not in common." A. Vaillant, *op. cit.*, p. 91. "This political fragmentation explains why the literary Convention signed by the Croats and the Serbs in Vienna in 1850 remained a pious hope." H. Boissin, *La Littérature Serbo-Croate*, in *Europe*, No. 435-436 (1965), p. 36.

43   Cf. Lj. Jonke, *Osnovni problemi jezika hrvatske književnosti u 19. stoljeću*, in Radovi Slavenskog Instituta, No. 2, Zagreb 1958, 75-91. Various aspects of the development of the Croatian literary language in the 19th century are examined by Z. Vince, *Ljudevit Gaj i hrvatski književni jezik*, in Jezik 1 (1972/73), 1-11. Id. *Putovima hrvatskoga književnog jezika*, Zagreb, Liber, 1978,˙195-270. Cf. also D. Brozović, *O ulozi Ljudevita Gaja u završnoj etapi hrvatske jezične unifikacije*, Institut za Hrvatsku Povijest, Radovi 3 (1973), 35-63. Lj. Jonke, *Ljudevit Gaj kao višestruki pobjednik*, in Jezik (1975/76), 67-79.

44   R. Katičić, *O početku novoštokavskoga hrvatskoga jezičnog standarda*, in Filologija (1978), p. 180.

45   Elements of the Czech language are already found in literary Croatian in the sixteenth century (Š. Budinić, Zadar) and then in the eighteenth century with the *kaj* writer Adam Patačić, and finally at the time of Illyrianism in the nineteenth century. It was during this last period that Croatian came under a powerful influence of the Czech language and a great many Behemianisms invaded and inundated literary Croatian. The Croatian alphabet, too, was often modelled on the Czech alphabet. In 1583 the Zadar poet Šime Budinić borrowed from the so-called Hussite Czech alphabet, named after Jan Hus, two letters to transcribe the phonemes /č/ and /ž/; this was also done by Pavao Vitezović who rejected digraphs and, above all, as the continuator of Vitezović, by Lj. Gaj, who, in 1830, in his book *Kratka osnova horvatsko-slavenskog pravopisanja* (A Brief Basis for a Croatian-Slavonic Orthography)¦ proposed and obtained the acceptance of the use of the single letters č, ž, š, after the Czech model to transcribe the corresponding phonemes /č/, /ž/ and /š/. The letter ě (cornute e) which in Croatian orthography sometimes represented *je* and sometimes *ije* throughout the nineteenth century was also borrowed from the Czech. Similarly the sign ć was borrowed from the Polish script. The reform of Gaj also helped the Slovenes to solve the age-old problem of Slovene orthography by the acceptance of *Gajica* (Gaj's ortho-

graphy). Janez Blajvajs (1808-1881) adopted Gaj's orthography for his paper *Novice* (1839-1846). Cf. T.Z. Gasinski, *West Slavic influences in the Language of Šime Budinić, Croatian 16th Century Writer,* Stanford University M.A. thesis, Stanford, 1962; cf. also T.Z. Gasinski, *A new Look at the Question of the Czech Linguistic Influences in the Language of Šime Budinić,* in Journal of Croatian Studies, New York, Vol. IX-X, 1968-69, 174-181. Cf. Tomo Maretić, *Ruske i češke riječi u književnom hrvatskom jeziku,* in Rad, JAZU, No. 108 (1892), 1-33. Lj. Jonke, *Češki jezični elementi u hrvatskosprpskom književnom jeziku,* in *Radovi zavoda za slavensku filologiju,* Zagreb, 1963, No. 5, p. 35-46.

46 M. Weingart et al., *Slovanské spisovné jazyky v době přitomné,* Prague, 1937, p. 5.

47 By its precision and linguistic value and the importance it attaches to the literary language, this work surpasses all the dictionaries of the period, namely A.F. Richter - A.J. Ballmann - R. Fröhlich, *Illyrisch-deutsches und Deutsch-illyrisches Handwörterbuch,* Wien, 1839-40. 2 vol.; this dictionary is based on J. Voltić's *Ricsoslovnik,* a trilingual Croat-Italian-German dictionary published in Vienna in 1803. J. Drobnić, *Mali ilirsko-njemačko-talijanski rječnik* (Vienna, 1846-1849). I.R.A. Veselić - Fröhlich, *Rječnik ilirskoga i njemačkoga jezika* (Vienna, 1853 and 1854).

48 Lj. Jonke, *Šulekova briga o hrvatskoj naučnoj terminologiji,* Zbornik radova Filozofskog fakulteta u Zagrebu, knj. II (1954), 67-81; also *Slavenske pozajmljenice u Šulekovu Rječniku znanstvenog nazivlja,* Zbornik radova Fil. fak. Zagreb, knj. III, 1965, 71-82. The work *Juridisch-politische Terminologie für die slavischen Sprachen Oesterreichs deutsch-kroatische, serbische und slovenische Ausgabe,* Vienna, 1853, had a certain importance in the development of official legal and political terminology in the nineteenth century. This voluminous terminological dictionary (about 700 pages) was compiled by the Yugoslav section of a special commission set up in 1849. The members of this commission were V.S. Karadžić, F. Miklošić, M. Dolenc, D. Demeter, B. Petranović and M. Mažuranić. The German words are arranged alphabetically and the Croatian, Serb and Slovene lexical equivalents are given in parallel. In the same year (1853) was printed in Vienna *Obći gradjanski zakonik* (the Civil Code) containing the basic Croat legal and political terminology. I. Filipović's *Neues Wörterbuch der kroatischen und deutschen Sprache. Zum Gebrauche für Juristen, Beamte . . .,* was published in Zagreb in 1869. The first Croatian juridical journal *Pravdonoša* was edited in Zadar in 1851 by A. Kuzmanić.

It should be also noted that the Croatian legal terminology is different from the Serbian; we cite only a few very current examples: Cr. *rastava* 'divorce' Sb. *razvod*; Cr. *kazneni zakonik* 'penal code' Sb. *krivični zakon*; Cr. *skrbnik* 'guardian' Sb. *staraoc*; Cr. *nagodba* 'agreement' Sb. '*poravnanje*'; Cr. *vjerovnik* 'creditor' Sb. *poverilac*; Cr. *vlasništvo* 'property' Sb. *svojina*; Cr.

pristanak 'accord' Sb. *saglasnost*; Cr. *zahtjev* 'claim' Sb. *tražbina*; Cr. *globa* 'fine, penalty, mulct' Sb. *novčana kazna*; Cr. *odluka* 'verdict' Sb. *rešenje*; Cr. *osuda* 'decree, judgement' Sb. *presuda*; Cr. *utok (priziv)* 'appeal' Sb. *žalba* (in Croatian *žalba* is 'complaint'); Cr. *(sudbena) rasprava* 'hearing, trial' Sb. *(sudski) pretres*; Cr. *ovrha* 'seizure' Sb. *uzapćenje*; Cr. *premetačina (redarstvena)* 'search (of a house)' Sb. *(policiski) pretres*; Cr. *izgred (prekršaj)* 'breach of the peace, violation of a law' Sb. *istup*; Cr. *prosvjed* 'protest' Sb. *protest*; Cr. *stanarina* 'a rent' Sb. *kirija*; Cr. *istražitelj* 'investigator' Sb. *islednik*; Cr. *sudac istražitelj* 'judge hearing a criminal case' Sb. *isledni sudija*; Cr. *ovrhovoditelj* 'distraining officer of the court' Sb. *izvršilac*; Cr. *provalnik* 'housebreaker, burglar' Sb. *obijač*; Cr. *kleveta, osvada* 'slander, defamation' Sb. *obeda*; Cr. *svrha* 'purpose, view' Sb. *cilj*; Cr. *urota* 'conspiracy, plot' Sb. *zavera*; Cr. *urotnik* 'conspirator, plotter' Sb. *zaverenik*; Cr. *zaruke* 'engagement, betrothal' Sb. *veridba*; Cr. *zapis, legat* 'legacy, bequest' Sb. *zaveštaj*; Cr. *zaklada* 'endowment' Sb. *zaveštanje*; Cr. *oporučiti (oporučno ostaviti)* 'to bequeath' Sb. *zaveštati*; Cr. *službem* (adj.) 'official' Sb. *zvaničan*; Cr. *ostavština* 'legacy' Sb. *zaostavština*, etc.

49 The German sociolinguist Heinz Kloss claims that the technical prose (*Sachprosa* or *Zweckprosa*) or the jargon peculiar to a trade (*Fachprosa*) are, in our time, more important in the elaboration of a language than poetry or the most elevated literary prose (cf. H. Kloss, *Völker, Sprachen, Mundarten* in *Europa Ethnica*, 26, Wien, 4, 78, p. 146-155).

50 Cf. Lj. Jonke, *Književni jezik u teoriji i praksi*, Zagreb, 1965; second edition, 261-271.

51 Cf. P. Skok, *O jezičnoj kulturi*, Jezik, 2 (1952), especially the chapter *Jezična kultura i purizam* (pp. 36-38).

52 Cf. Lj. Jonke, *Veberove zasluge za naš književni jezik*, in *Rad*, No. 309 (1956). Cf. also Z. Vince, *Putovima Hrvatskoga Književnog Jezika*, Zagreb, 1978, 403-602.

53 M. Mamić, *Hrvatski ustavnopravni jezik u 2. polovici 19. stoljeća*, in *Rasprave zavoda za jezik*, 6-7 (1980-1981), 163-226.

54 Cf. Lj. Jonke, *Daničićev prilog normi i kodifikaciji hrvatskog književnog jezika* (Daničić's Contribution to the Standardization and Codification of the Croatian Literary Language , in Zbornik o Djuri Daničiću (1981), 45.

55 Cf. Gerald G. Govorchin, *Pravaštvo and the Croatian National Issue*, in East European Quarterly, 1978, 12 (1), 57-68.

56 Lj. Jonke, *Hrvatski književni jezik 19. i 20. stoljeća*, Zagreb, 1971, p.176.

57   Cf. T. Maretić, *Crtice o rječniku naše Akademije*, in Ljetopis JAZU, 31, Zagreb, 1916, 67-68.

58   R. Katičić, *O početku novoštokavskoga hrvatskoga jezičnog standarda*, in Filologija (1978), p. 18o. Z. Vince, *Norma u hrvatskom književnom jeziku potkraj 19. stoljeća*, in Jezik, 30 (1982), 51-57, 80-85.

59   "In developing itself, the Serbian literary language had to constitute the whole abstract vocabulary which the popular language did not provide. It did so by resorting freely to borrowing, modelling itself on Russian, . . . and retaining from Slavonic and Russian tradition the words it needed . . . But on the whole, modern Serbian is full of Russian words and this is not realised; it is only the history of the vocabulary which shows that words which seem perfectly Serbian are no older than the end of the eighteenth century . . . The literary language adopted them in abundance and their use has spread to all Serbs." (A. Vaillant, op. cit., p. 87).

60   "A historian of Šerbian literature such as Skerlich finds no breach between the literary language of the beginning of the nineteenth century and modern literary language; he sees a language which has progressively purified itself as a Serbian literature has developed." (A. Vaillant, ibid., p. 87).

61   Rasio Dunatov, *A Sociolinguistic Analysis of the Recent Controversy Concerning the Croatian/Serbian Standard Language(s)*, in American Contributions to the Eighth International Congress of Slavists in Zagreb—Ljubljana", vol. 1, p. 259.

62   For the phonological opposition /-je-/ : /-i-/ in Croatian cf. *Hrvatski Pravopis*, London, 1972, p. 40. Cf. also Z. Bjelanović, *O nesvršenim glagolima tipa dotjecati* (On the imperfective verbs of the type *dotjecati*), Jezik, 19:1 (1971), 19-26.

63   Cf. Maretić, *Gramatika i stilistika hrvatskoga ili srpskoga književnog jezika*, second edition, Zagreb, 1931, 54-56. Cf. also V. Putanec, *Neki noviji hiperjekavizmi*, Jezik 11 (1963-1964), 75-79. J. Hamm, *Sekundarno ije na zapadnom hrvatskom području*, in Jezik 2 (1952), 39-45.

64   Cf. *Hrvatski Pravopis* (Croatian Orthography), London, 1972, 33-43.

65   Cf. L. Weissgerber, *Sprachenrecht und europäische Einheit*, Köln, Westdeutscher Verlag, 1959.

66   Cf. Lj. Jonke, *Razvoj hrvatskoga književnog jezika u 20. stoljeću*, in Radovi Zavoda za slavensku filologiju, 10, 99-110. Id. *Hrvatski književni*

155

jezik 19. i 20. stoljeća (The Croatian literary language in the 19th and 20th centuries), Matica hrvatska, Zagreb, 1971. V. Gudkov, *O različijah meždu dvumja variantami serbo-hrvatskogo literaturnogo jazyka*, in Sovetskoe slavjanovedenie, 3 (1965), 52-59. A.W. Wainmann, *The Differences in Lexical, Syntactical and Morphological Usage between the Eastern and Western Variants of Serbo-Croat ...*, in Canadian Papers presented at the IV International Congress of Slavists in Prague, 1968; D. Petranović, *Prilog karakterizaciji razlika izmedu ekavskog i ijekavskog književnog jezika*, in Zbornik za filologiju i lingvistiku, 13 (1970), 71-76. H. Kuna, *Istorijska podloga varijantskih razlika srpskohrvatskog standardnog jezika*, in Književnost i jezik, 4 (1975), 19-33.

67   "Script is identical with religion and religion is identical with national feeling, because among the Slavs religious feeling has always been closely linked to national feeling . . . But the dualism of alphabets and scripts persists, which in practice is as troublesone as a diversity of language . . . This creates a division which remains fairly wide in a country where Yugoslav feeling and the desire for union are evident." (A. Vaillant, *L'écriture et la psychologie des peuples*, Paris, 1964, p. 307). On the subject of dual scripts Simeon Potter writes: "Today, therefore, the line of demarcation runs between Belgrade and Zagreb, dividing Yugoslavia into two. Indeed, the Slavonic world as a whole is divided on this significant issue." (*Modern Linguistics*, London, 1957, p. 57).

68   "It is this top layer of the literary vocabulary which best reflects the civilisation to which a language belongs. Now, the Croatian countries and the Serbian countries belong precisely to two different worlds; the former are part of Central Europe, the latter of the Balkan community." (B. Ungegaun, *Le calque dans les langues slaves*, RES XII (1932), p. 24.) Cf. also Charles E. Bidwell, *Language Dialect and Nationality in Yugoslavia*, Human Relations, London, Vol. 15, No. 3 (1962), 217-225.

69   For special and technical Croatian dictionaries see B. Franolić, *A Selective Bibliography of Croatian Dictionaries*, N.E.L., Paris (in print).

70   Cf. J. Šetka, *Hrvatska kršćanska terminologija* (Croatian Christian Terminology), Split, 1976, second edition, 366 p. Cf. the report by B. Franolić in Lingua, Amsterdam, Vol. 29 (1972), 95-100.

71   Cf. *Hrvatski Latinisti*, Zagreb, Vol. I (1969), Vol. II (1970), in the collection *Pet stoljeća hrvatske književnosti* (Five centuries of Croatian literature), published by Matica hrvatska—Zora. Cf. also the bibliographical work of Šime Jurić, *Opera scriptorum latinorum natione croatorum . . . Zagrabiae* 1968 I-III, which records the Latin works written up to the first half of the nineteenth century. V. Gortan—V. Vratović, *The Basic Characteristics of Croatian Latinity*, in Humanistica Lovaniensia 20 (1971), 37-38; V. Vratović,

L'Esprit national et international de la littérature latine croate, in Acta Conventus Neo-Latini Lovaniensis, Leuwen University Press — Wilhelm Fink Verlag, München, 1973, 687-691.

72   Cf. R. Auty, *Pannonian parallels and divergencies: thoughts on the history of the Croatian and Hungarian literary languages,* in Filologija 8, 29-36 (1978), Zagreb. Auty presents a brief survey of the Croatian literary language in the 18th and 19th centuries in the context of a desire for *Sprachanschluss* and points to parallel developments in Hungarian. I. Nyomárkay, *Deutsche Lehnübersetzungen im Kroatischen und im Ungarischen,* in Studia Slavica Academiae Scientiarum Hungaricae, 22 (1976), Nos 3-4, 301-312.

73   Cf. A. Škaljić, *Turcizmi u narodnom govoru i narodnoj književnosti Bosne i Hercegovine,* Sarajevo, 1957.   A. Knežević, *Die Turzismen in der Sprache der Kroaten und Serben,* Meisenheim am Glan, Hain, 1962, 506 pp. A. Škaljić, *Turcizmi u srpskohrvatskom jeziku,* Sarajevo, 1965.

74   *Aljamia* (Arabic *al adjamiyya*), a term used for the writing of non-Arabic languages in Arabic characters, was applied in Bosnia to Slavic, just as in Spain it was applied to Romance or in the Northern region of Nigeria to Hausa. Another Slavic language, Belorussian, has been periodically transcribed in Arabic characters by local Moslems who represent the Slavicised descendants of former Tartar invaders. The Arabic sense is 'non-Arab', hence 'barbarous'. The literature in *aljamía* which has been preserved is therefore termed *aljamiado.* The printing of *aljamiado* books started in the very last period of Turkish rule in Bosnia. Altogether, about forty books were printed in Arabic but the last one, *Fikhulibadat,* by Mohamed Sejd Serdarević, was printed as recentrly as 1941 in Sarajevo. (Cf. A. Hadžijahić, *Hrvatska muslimanska književnost prije 1878,* Sarajevo, 1938.   A. Nametak, *Gaševićev bosanski Mevlud,* Sarajevo, 1936.   F. Karihman, *Los escritores croatas de religión musulmana,* in Studia Croatica, 46-47 (1972), 152-164.   F. Karihman, *Soj i Odžak Ehli-Islama,* The anthology of Croat poets of Moslem religion, München-Barcelona, 1974, 233 p.) — "Another European language once written in Arabic script by a Muslim minority is Croatian. From the 14th to late 19th century, Bosnia, Macedonia, and Southern Serbia formed part of the Ottoman empire. Most of the local nobility and landowners became Muslims, and they wrote their Croatian vernacular in Arabic script (adapted by diacritical marks to express Slavic sounds). The script, variously known as Arabica, Matufovica, or Aljamiado (as in Spain) was used for private correspondence as well as for literary purposes, but only some 40 works (mostly religious tracts, poems, and legends) were printed in Arabica." Hans H. Wellisch, *The Conversion of Scripts __ Its Nature, History and Utilization,* New York, 1978, John Willey & Sons, p. 117.

75   Cf. A. Nametak, *Rukopisni tursko-hrvatskosrpski rječnici, Građa za povijest književnosti hrvatske,* Vol. 29 (1968), 231-380, especially 361-380.

76   Cf. B. Franolić, *An Historical Outline of Croatian Lexicography*, in Die Welt der Slaven, Munich, XXVIII, 2 (1983), 286-306.

77   Cf. H. Šabanović, *Književnost Muslimana BiH na orijentalnim jezicima*, Svjetlost, Sarajevo, 1974.

78   Cf. also F. Karihman, *Los escritores croatas de religión musulmana*, in Studia Croatica, Buenos Aires, Vol. 46-47 (1972), 152-164.

79   For Italianisms in Croatian, cf. M. Hraste, *Strani elementi u hrvatskom ili srpskom narodnom i književnom jeziku*, in Radovi Slavenskog Instituta, Vol. 2, Zagreb, 1958, 43-58. S. Tagliavini, *Sugli elementi italiani del croato*, in Italia e Croazia, Rome, 1942, published by Reale Academia d'Italia, 377-454. Cf. also J. Jernej, *Sugli italianismi penetrati nel serbo-croato negli ultimi cento anni*, in Studia Romanica I, Zagreb, 1956, 58-72. Id. *Interferenze linguistiche sulle coste orientali del bacino adriatico*, in Boll. Atlante ling. Mediter. (1968-1970), No 10-12, 49-55.   G. Maver, *Parole croate di origine italiana o dalmatica*, in Archivum Romanicum, VI, 1922, 241-253. Ž. Muljačić, *Scambi lessicali tra l'Italia meridionale e la Croazia*. Abruzzo, VIII, Roma 1970, 1, 45-55.   Idem, *Noterelle lessicologiche*, in Ricerche slavistiche, XVII-XIX, Firenze 1973, 407-418.   Idem, *Contatti linguistici fra la Croazia e l'Italia centrale e meridionale*, in Atti del Congresso Internazionale sulle Relazioni fra le due Sponde adriatiche, ottobre 1971, Lecce 1973 (1975), 235-248.   Idem, *Su alcuni toscanismi antichi nel dialetto croato di Dubrovnik*, in Bollettino dell'Atlante Linguistico Mediterraneo, 13-15, 1971-1973, Firenze, 1976, 9-17. Idem, *Noterelle lessicali italo-croate*, in Italia linguistica nuova ed antica, vol. II, Galatina, Congedo Editore, 1978, 197-203.

For Germanisms, cf. H. Striedter-Temps, *Deutsche Lehnwörter im Serbokroatischen*, Wiesbaden, 1958; E. Schneeweiss, *Die deutschen Lenhwörter im Serbo-kroatischen*, Berlin 1960; M. Rammelmeyer, *Die deutschen Lehnübersetzungen im Serbokroatischen*, *Beiträge zur Lexicologie und Wortbildung*, Wiesbaden, Steiner, 1975.

80   For Croatian writers in the Italian language, cf. M. Zorić, *Zaboravljeno poglavlje iz hrvatske književne prošlosti: pisci talijanskog jezičnog izraza u Dalmaciji i Nikola Tommaseo*, in Kritika 11 (1970), 193-213. Nicolas Tommaseo, a Dalmatian of Šibenik, after spending all his youth in Italy, his adopted country, was soon to pay tribute to his home country: in 1848 he composed a small volume called *Iskrice* (Sparks), a cycle of thirty-three prose poems, inspired by Lamennais's *Paroles d'un croyant* and overflowing with love for Dalmatia and its people. Some other eminent Italian philologists: A. Mussafia, G. Bartoli, G. Goidánich, G. Vidossich, were also born in Croatia. (Cf. Tullio De Mauro, *Idee e ricerche linguistiche nella cultura italiana*, Bologna, 1980.) Even in the 20th century V. Nazor wrote his allegorical epic *Brundo the Bear* (1915) in parallel in Italian and Croatian (*Medvjed Brundo*). It is a satirical poem

whose characters are drawn from the animal world. Just as Edmond Rostand's *Chanteclair* symbolises the French nation, so the old bear *Brundo* and the young wolf *Vukan* symbolise the Croatian people. "In short, in the languages, beside the purely genealogical kinship, one should take into account a cultural affinity which is the result of all kinds of exchanges established among the peoples (of Europe) whatever their origin may be." (B. Migliorini, *Convergences linguistiques en Europe*, Synthèses, Bruxellses, No 47, April 1950). "Thus a language may be defined by the vocabulary used and by the way the elements of this vocabulary are varied and arranged in groups." (A. Meillet)

81 "Slovene has exerted an appreciable influence on literary Croatian; in particular it has supplied a good many Slovene loan translations", B. Unbegaun, *Le Calque dans les langues slaves*, RES, p. 30; see, for the whole question, the article by A. Breznik, *Vpliv slovenskih slovarjev na srbsko-hrvatske*, in Časopis za slovenski jezik, književnost in zgodovino, VIII, 1931, 16-67.

82 Cf. H. Kloss, *Die Entwicklung neuer germanischer Kultursprachen von 1800-1950*, München, 1952, p. 166.

83 Cf. I. Popović, *Grčko-srpske lingvističke studije* II (Greco-Serbian linguistic studies), in Zbornik Radova S.A.N. Vizant. Inst. Jugosl. (1955), No 3 III-7. It can be said in general that the linguistic influence of the Byzantines on the Serbs (and more rarely on the Croats) was subsequent to the first Bulgarian and Macedonian-Hellenic exchanges. The author (I. Popović) thinks that the action of Greek on Serbian must be earlier than the twelfth century, that is to say before the first Old Serbian literary texts. But it became considerable only around the thirteenth century and the following centuries. Once started, it did not cease until well after the fall of Byzantium and of mediaeval Serbia. Cf. also Max Vasmer, *Die griechischen Lenhwörter im Serbokroatischen*, Berlin, 1944, 145 p. Greek influence on Croatian was not significant and loan-words in Croat borrowed directly from Greek are not numerous (e.g. *teka* 'exercise book'). Some popular loan-words of Greek origin are common both to Croats and Serbs, e.g. *anđeo* 'angel', *đavao* 'devil', *đak* 'pupil', *miris* 'fragrance, scent', *krevet* 'bed', Cr. *jeftin* (Sb. *jevtin*) 'cheap'; *temelj* 'foundation', *komad* 'piece'; *komad* assumed the old meaning of *kruh* 'piece' which in turn in Croat assumed the meaning of *hljeb* 'bread'. Some are used mainly in Serbian: *drum* 'road', *ćelija* 'cell', *hiljada* 'thousand', *krîn* 'lily', *hartija* 'paper', *kamila* 'camel', *stomak* 'stomach', *kondir* 'pitcher, jug', *pihtije* 'aspic', *skiptar* 'sceptre', *patos* 'floor', *poklisar* 'envoy', *talas* 'wave', *tiganj* 'frying pan', *trpezarija* 'dining room', *rovito jaje* 'a soft boild egg'; especially the words used in Byzantine Church terminology: *ćivot* (*kivot*) 'box or case', *eparhija* 'diocese', *monah* 'monk', *ktitor* 'founder of a monastery', *kaluđer* 'monk', *manastir* 'monastery', *kandilo* 'hanging light before an icon', *parastos* 'requiem', *paroh* 'vicar', *patarica* 'a bishop's crosier', *prota* 'vicar', *iguman* 'abbot', *dóhija*, 'monastery kitchen', *putir*

'chalice', *tipik* 'a book of monastic rules', *hrisovulja* 'document', etc. There are also linguistic calques of Greek origin to be found in Serbian such as *sedmica* Gk. hebdomas=Rom. *septimana* Cr. *tjedan*, or neologisms, such as *bioskop* 'cinema' Cr. *kino*. A particular duality appears regarding learned loan words from Greek, borrowed roughly before mid-nineteenth century. The Croats received these loan-words from Greek as they were rendered in the church (and later humanist) Latin of Central Europe; e.g. Cr. *biskup* < Lat. *episcopus* < Gk. *epískopos* > Sb. *episkop*, Cr. *ciborij* < Lat. *ciborium* < Gk. *kibórion*. The Serbs in direct contact with the Byzantine cultural tradition adapted the Modern Greek pronunciation directly to their own phonetic system. Thus the following regular divergences occur between the Croatian and the Serbian versions of many Greek loans:

Greek *eta* is borrowed by the Serbs as *i*, by the Croats as *e* (Gk. *Athênai* Sb. *Atina*, Cr. *Atena* 'Athens'; Gk. *klêros* Sb. *klir* Cr. *kler* 'clergy'), etc.

The diphtongs *eu* and *au* become respectively *eu* and *au* to the Croats, *ev* and *av* to the Serbs (Gk. *Europe* Sb. *Evropa* Cr. *Europa*; Gk. *eunoûchos* Sb. *evnuh* Cr. *eunuh* 'eunuch'; Latin *Augustus* Cr. *August*, Gk. *Augoustos* Sb. *Avgust* 'August'; Gk. *Maûros* Lat. *Maurus* Sb. *Mavar* Cr. *Maur* 'Moor'; *Zeus* Sb. *Zevs* Cr. *Zeus*.

Sometimes the initial epsilon of the Greek diphtong *eu* was rendered as *je* in Serbian and as *e* in Croat (Gk. *euangélion* Lat. *evangelium* Sb. *jevanđelje* Cr. *evanđelje* 'evangel').

Beta becomes *v* in Serbian, *b* in Croatian (*Bethlehem* Sb. *Vitlejem* Cr. *Betlehem* 'Bethlehem'; *Byzantion* Sb. *Vizant(ija)* Cr. *Bizant* 'Byzantium'; *bárbaros* Sb. *varvarin* Cr. *barbarin*; *labýrinthos* Sb. *lavirint* Cr. *labirint* 'labyrinth').

Chi becomes *h* in Serbian, *k* in Croat (*Chronika* Sb. *hronika* Cr. *kronika;* *Christos* Sb. *Hristos* Cr. Krist 'Christ'; *chaos* Sb. *haos* Cr. *kaos* 'chaos'), etc.

Kappa before front vowel becomes *c* in Croatian but remains *k* in Serbian (*okeanós* Sb. *okean,* Cr. *ocean* 'ocean'; *Kypros* Sb. *Kipar,* Cr. *Cipar* 'Cyprus'; *kédros* 'cedar' Sb. *kedar* Cr. *cedar; kéntauros* 'centaur' Sb. *kentaur,* Cr. *centaur*), etc.

The *spiritus asper* becomes h in Croatian loans, but does not appear in Serbian loans (*historia* Sb. *istorija,* Cr. *historija* 'history'; or appears in Serbian as *j*; e.g. *Hellas* Sb. *Jelada,* Cr. *Helada; hairetikos* Sb. *jeretik,* Cr. *heretik; hairesis* Sb. *jeres,* Cr. *hereza; hierárches* Sb. *jerarhija* Cr. *hijerarhija,* etc.

Intervocalic *s* becomes *z* in Croatian loans, remaining *s* in Serbian (Gk. *kósmos* Sb. *kosmos,* Cr. *kozmos; Hierousalêm* Sb. *Jerusalim,* Cr. *Jeruzalem.*

Intervocalic *phi* was reflected as *v* in Serbian, as *p* in Croatian (*Stéfanos* Sb. *Stevan,* Cr. *Stjepan*).

Intervocalic *gamma* was rendered in Serbian as *đ (đj)*, in Croat as *g* (*leitourgía* Sb. *liturđija,* M. Lat. *liturgia* Cr. *liturgija; magike* Sb. *mađija* Lat. *magica* Cr. *magija*).

Intervocalic *ti* of the suffix *-atia* did not change in Serbian, but became *c* in Croat (Gk. *demokratia* Sb. *demokratija* Cr. *demokracija* 'democracy'; *aristokratia* Sb. *aristokratija* Cr. *aristokracija* 'aristocracy'). Consequently

160

we have in Serbian *birokratija* 'bureaucracy', *diplomatija* 'diplomacy', in Croatian *birokracija, diplomacija*, etc.

Greek names ending in *-cles: Pericles, Sophocles, Themistocles* end in Serbian in *-kle: Perikle, Sofokle, Temistokle* and in Croatian in *-klo: Periklo, Sofoklo, Temistoklo.*

One of the most productive verbal suffixes in Serbian *-isati* is of Greek origin to which in Croat corresponds *-irati* of Franco-German provenance. (Cf. S. Mønnesland, *Loanwords in the Two Variants of Serbo-Croatian*, in Scando-Slavica *19 [1973], 197-205*].

84   Cf. K. Gutschmidt, *The part played by Church Slavonic in the formation of the Bulgarian and the Serbian literary languages* (in Russian), in Voprosy Yazykoznaniya, S.S.S.R. (1969) No. 6, 71-82.

85   For loan-translations in literary Croatian cf. B. Unbegaun, op. cit. R.E.S. XII (1932), 23-29. M. Rammelmeyer, *Die deutsche Lehnübersetzungen im Serbokroatischen*, Wiesbaden, Steiner, 1975.

86   Cf. B. Franolić's   review of *Leksik Prezimena Socijalističke Republike Hrvatske*, in Die Welt der Slawen, Heft 2 (1981).

87   On the subject of calques in these Slav languages, Unbegaun concludes: "This is a usage, if not an evil, which is today common to all Central Europe and which reached its height with the Magyars. People have talked for a long time of the lingusitic community of the Balkan world, a community which asserts itself by the general characteristics of vocabulary and syntax and, even of morphology. But if one were some day to try to determine a similar community for Central Europe it would be the process of calques which would be its most characteristic indication." (B. Unbegaun, op. cit. p. 48). Cf. also R. Auty, *Sources and Methods of Lexical Enrichment in the Slavonic Language — Revivals of the Early Nineteenth Century*, The Slavic World, The Hague, 1970, 41-52. Id., *Problèmes de la formation des langues littéraires Slaves,* R.E.S. XLV, 7-18.

88   Cf. S. Babić, *Htijenja i ostvarenja Novosadskog dogovora,* Jezik 15 (1967-68), 3-13; M. Moguš, *Varijante prelaze puke okvire komunikativnosti,* Jezik 16 (1968-69), 1-4; Z. Malić, *Pismeno i usmeno komuniciranje,* Jezik, ib. 6-8. S. Babić, *Lingvističko određenje hrvatskoga književnog jezika,* Jezik 18 (1970-71), 129-137.

89   Cf. D. Brozović, *O problemima varijanata,* in Jezik, 13 (1965-66), 34-46. D. Brozović, *Standardni jezik,* Zagreb, 1970. It may be noted that *Gramatika i stilistika hrvatskoga ili srpskoga književnog jezika* (Zagreb, 1931), regarded as the best Serbo-Croat grammar, takes no account of the Croatian literary language, but draws the examples and citations in support of its normative rules solely from folk-poetry and folk-tales, or in other words from

village folklore, and from the "canonical" writings of V. Karadžić and Đ. Daničić. The same could be said of the Dictionary of the Croatian language by Broz-Iveković (Zagreb, 1901, 2 vol.), while the Dictionary of the Academy of Zagreb (1880 and following years) disregards four centuries of *kaj* literature and scarcely mentions, or even passes over in silence, the major Croatian writers of the nineteenth century, such as Šenoa, Kumičić, Gjalski, etc. (Cf. P. Šegedin, *Pitanja hrvatskog književnog jezika*, Encyclopaedia Moderna, No. 13 (1970), 58-63). A great part of this Dictionary was already out of date before the publication was completed: the Dictionary's first volume had been published in 1880, its last in 1976. It also omits the technical words which a writer may have to use according to the nature of his work. Underlying this attitude is the romantic concept, later adopted by positivist research, that everything created by the people is, by the mere fact of being popular, more beautiful, truer and more authentic, in a word, more valid, than anything which is artistic and therefore artificial. This romantic assumption is mainly manifested in the admiration of folk-poetry and folk-tales ("the treasure of the people") and in the fascination of the neo-što vernacular of the Herzegovinian villages.

90 J. Lyons, *Language, Meaning & Context*, Fontana Paperbacks, 1981, p. 49.

91 Cf. the article by S. Babić cited in note 88, Jezik 15.

92 Cf. R. Bošković, *O leksičkoj i stilskoj diferencijaciji srpskoga i hrvatskoga književnog jezika*, in Naš Jezik, 3 (1935), 277-282. Cf. also J. Benešić, *Gramatika jezika chorwatskiego czyli serbskiego*, Warszawa, 1937, chapter: *Serbizmy i kroatyzmy*, p. 233-278.

93 The full title: Petar Guberina-Kruno Krstić, *Razlike između hrvatskoga i srpskoga književnog jezika*, Zagreb, 1940, 1-218. See also the report by B. Jurišić in Nastavni Vjesnik, *1942, 268-281.*

94 B. Vančik, in Hrvatski književni list, 2 (Zagreb, 1969), No. 10 of 31 January, 1969.

95 Cf. Z. Vince, *Riječka Filološka škola*, in Putovima hrvatskoga književnog jezika, Zagreb, 1978, 403-470.

96 Cf. Stj. Babić, *Zur Frage des Systems in der kroatischen Wortbildung*, in Zeitschrift für Slavische Philologie, Band XXXVI, Heft 1 (1971), 92-107. Id., *Sustav u mocijskoj tvorbi u suvremenom hrvatskom književnom jeziku*, in Slavica Helvetica, *Colloquium Slavicum Basiliense*, Gedenkschrift für Hildegard Schroeder, Hg. von H. Riggenbach. . ., Bern-Frankrut/Main-Las Vegas, 1981, 33-46.

97   Cf. I. Pederin, *The Croatian Language at the Beginning of the Industrial Period* (in Croat), in Zadarska Revija, 5, 1971, 340-351.

98   Cf. B. Franolić, *L'Intégration des suffixes d'origine française et étrangère dans le système suffixal croate,* in Lingua, 27 (1971), 355-366.

99   Cf. B. Franolić, *L'Adaptation des verbes d'origine française en croate,* in Die Welt der Slaven, Heft 1 (1980), 153-160.

100   Cf. B. Franolić, *L'Adaptation des mots composés et des locutions d'origine française en croate,* in Linguistics, 69, The Hague (May 1971), 33-43.

101   Cf. B. Franolić, *Le Traitement des phonèmes /r, l, m, n/ précédés d'une consonne à la finale absolue des mots d'emprunt français en croate,* in Die Welt der Slaven (1972) XVII, Heft 2, 268-279. Id., *La Structure interne du mot d'emprunt français en croate,* in Annali Dell'Istituto Universitario Orientale, Napoli (1979), vol. XX-XXI, 85-102.

102   Cf. B. Franolić, *Adaptation secondaire ou la dérivation des emprunts d'origine française en croate,* in Lingua 40 (1976), 247-261. Id. *L'Adaptation morphologique des adjectifs d'origine française en croate,* in Die Welt der Slaven (1972) XVII, Heft 1, 18-26.

103   Cf. B. Franolić, *L'emprunt et le calque syntaxique et phraséologique en croate,* in Die Welt der Slaven, Heft 2 (1979), 405-417.

104   Cf. B. Franolić, *L'Intégration morphologique des mots d'emprunt français en croate,* in Lingua (1969), vol. 22, 133-159. Id., *La Déclinaison des substantifs croates d'origine française qui se terminent par -e, -i, -o, -u,* in Annali Dell'Istituto Universitario Orientale, Napoli (1976), vol. XVIII (1975), 155-160. For French influence in Croatia, see B. Franolić, *L'Influence de la langue française en Croatie,* Paris, Nouvelles Editions Latines, 1975; Id., *Les mots d'emprunt français en croate,* Paris, NEL, 1976.

105   Cf. T. Prpić, *Nekoliko rusizama novijega vremena,* in Jezik I (1952/53), 87-89; Id. *Još nekoliko rusizama,* in Jezik, 5 (1956/57), 20-24.

106   For English loanwords in Croatian, see R. Filipović, *The Phonemic Analysis of English Loan-words in Croatian,* Zagreb, 1960.

106a   Aldo Scaglione, *The Rise of National Languages: East and West,* in The Emergence of National Languages, Ravenna, 1984. P. 13.

107   Cf. Ch. Cviić, *Spellbound,* in Index, Vol. 2, No. 1, London, 1973, 127-128.

108   V. Meier, *Yugoslavia's National Question*, in Problems of Communism, March-April 1983, p. 57.

109   Lj. Jonke, *Hrvatski književni jezik danas*, Zagreb, 1971, p. 115, 119.

110   R. Dunatov, *A Sociolinguistic Analysis of the Recent Controversy Concerning the Croatian/Serbian Language(s)*, in American Contributions to the Eighth International Congress of Slavists in Zagreb-Ljubljana, 3-9 IX 1978, Vol. I, p. 260.

111   Ch. Spalatin, *Serbo-Croatian or Serbian and Croatian?* in Journal of Croatian Studies, Vol. VII-VIII, New York (1966/67), p. 5.

112   Cf. M. Kmecl, *O preživetju jezika*, in Bomo preživeli?, Celje, 1982, 125-135. Cf. also the articles of the Slovenian poets and writers: Ciril Zlobec in Delo (11. August 1983), Tone Partljič, in Delo (18 August 1983), Janez Menart, in Delo (2 Sept. 1983).

113   See the Declaration on the Name and Status of the Croatian Literary Language, of 15 March, 1967 (*Deklaracija o nazivu i položaju hrvatskoga književnog jezika*). In March 1967 some hundred Croatian intellectuals presented a resolution claiming complete equality between the Serbian and Croatian languages. This move was a bombshell. The signatories spoke in the name of the Association of Writers of the Republic of Croatia and eighteen other Croatian cultural and scientific institutions. Most of them were members of the League of Communists. They included the greatest contemporary Croatian writer, Miroslav Krleža, a member of the Central Committee of the Communist Party of Croatia.

114   Cf. Zagreb daily Vjesnik, 9th February 1971.

115   V. Meier, ibidem, p. 54.

116   Cf. Ľubomír[1] Ďurovič, *Slovak*, in *The Slavic Literary Languages: Formation and Development*, Yale Concilium on International and Area Studies, New Haven, 1980, p.

117   V. Meier, ibidem, p. 53.

118   Cf. Kenneth E. Naylor, *The Eastern Variant of Serbo-Croatian as the Lingua Communis of Yugoslavia*, in Folia Slavica, 1-3 (December 1978).

119   Cf. *Ne znam tvoj jezik*, in Belgrade weekly NIN, 28. Nov. 1982, p. 20, and *Zboruvate li makedonski?* in NIN, 15 January 1984, p. 16.

120   Cf. B. Franolić, *Language Policy and Language Planning in Yugoslavia with Special Reference to Croatian and Macedonian*, in Lingua 51 (1980), 55-72.

121   V. Meier, ibidem, p. 51.

122   H.G. Lunt, *The Creation of Standard Macedonian*, in Anthropological Linguistics, 1:5, 22 (1959).

123   V. Meier, ibidem, p. 54.

124   Cf. *Hrvatski književni jezik i pitanje varijanata* (The Croatian literary language and the question of variants), special edition of the periodical Kritika, vol. 1. Zagreb, 1969, 246 p. Cf. D. Brozović, *Rječnik jezika ili jezik Rječnika? Varijacije na temu varijanata*, special edition of the periodical Kritika, vol. 2, Zagreb 1969, 92 p. Cf. the discussion on the status of the Croatian language, which took place in the Writers' Union of Croatia, published in Telegram, Zagreb, 10/1969, No. 463 of 14 March, 1969. Cf. Thomas Magner, *Language and Nationalism in Yugoslavia*, Canadian Slavic Studies, Vol. I, No. 3, Fall 1967. S. Babić, *Za ravnopravnost, ali čega?* in Jezik, XV (1967/68), 134-147. Id. *Lingvističko određenje hrvatskoga književnog jezika*, in Jezik, XVIII (1970/71), 129-137. Id. *U lingvistici znanstvenost, u politici ravnopravnost*, in Jezik, XVI (1968/69), 52-60.

125   Cf. Communist daily *Borba*, 14 April 1961.

126   Cf. D. Brozović, *O jeziku u zakonima i o zakonu jezika*, in Jezik (1978/79), 13-23.

127   "But the problem in the country lies in another field; if there are two nations, Croatian and Serbian, it follows that each of them is entitled to call its language by its national name and to develop it as it thinks fit, regardless of the development of the sister language, and it is this right which has been denied to the Croatian language", writes Jean Morin in the Parisian review *Esprit*, February, 1970, p. 396. Cf. also M. Mostovac, *Le droit face au bilinguisme en droit yougoslave*, Proceedings of the Faculty of Law of the University of Ottawa, Ontario, Canada, 1969, 59-86. K. Spalatin, *Language and Politics in Yugoslavia in the light of the events which happened from March 17, 1967 to March 14, 1969*, in Journal of Croatian Studies, 1970-71, Vol. XI-XII, 83-104.

128   Cf. N.L. Karlovic, *Internal colonialism in a Marxist society: the case of Croatia*, in Ethnic and Racial Studies, Vol. 5, No. 3, London, July 1982, 276-299. Cf. also Louis-Jean Calvet, *Linguistique et Colonialisme*. Petit Traité de glottophagie, Payot, Paris, 1974.

129   Cf. Lj. Jonke, *Davičevo pogrešno rezoniranje o jeziku*, Jezik 3 (1966-67), 75-78. Cf. also Lj. Jonke, *S jezikom treba oprezno postupati*, in Hrvatski Književni Jezik Danas, p. 120. P. Herrity, *The Problem of Lexical Variants in the Standard Language in Bosnia-Hercegovina*, in Die Welt der Slaven, 27:77-89.

130   For language problems in Bosnia and Herzegovina, see Alija Isaković, *Nervoza u našem književnom jeziku*, in Odjek, Sarajevo XVIII 22 (1965), 15 November 1965, p. 52. D. Brozović, *O umjetnom usmjeravanju jezičnog razvoja*, in Telegram, VII, No. 297, 7 January, 1966. M. Hraste, *O trećoj varijanti hrvatsko-srpskog književnog jezika*, in Jezik 4 (1965-66), 106-113. Cf. also Collective writings in Odjek, No. 18 and 22, Sarajevo, 1968, and in Život, No. 11-12, Sarajevo, 1970. Cf. also the article by Čedo Kisić in Odjek, April 1970. V. Koroman, *Uvlake gredu — a postole stoje*, in Život, No. 11-12, 1970. V. Grubišić, *Bosansko-hercegovački nesporazumi*, in O Hrvatskom Jeziku, Chapter VII, 139-157, Rome 1975. On the Serbianisation of the official language used in the Yugoslav army, see the article *Nekoliko primjedaba uz mišljenje o porabi jezika u JNA* by the Slovene General Jaka Avšič, who denounces the linguistic imperialism of the Serbian military world. The article was published in Hrvatski Književni List, No. 19 and in Encyclopaedia Moderna, 5-12, Zagreb 1970, 111-119. V. Grbac, *Ravnopravni jezici u armiji*, Zagreb daily Vjesnik, 24 December, 1970, p. 7. Lj. Jonke, *O ravnopravnosti jezika u armiji*, in Hrvatski Književni Jezik Danas, p. 101-103. D. Ch. Šporer, *Politics and Nationalism within the Yugoslav People's Army*, The Journal of Croatian Studies, Vol. XX (1979), 118-131.

131   R. Dunatov, ibidem, p. 262.

132   Cf. Belgrade weekly NIN, 23 January 1983, p. 38.

133   Aspects of the language question in Bosnia and Herzegovina are the subject of several works: *O književnoj politici u Socijalističkoj Republici Bosni i Hercegovini*, Sarajevo, Oslobođenje 1975. *Mostarsko Savjetovanje o Književnom Jeziku*, Institut za jezik i književnost u Sarajevu, Sarajevo 1974. M. Šipka, *Jezički Savjetnik*, Svjetlost, Sarajevo 1976. *Pravopisna problematika u Bosni i Hercegovini*, Sarajevo, Institut za jezik i književnost, Odjeljenje za jezik, Radovi 3 (1976). Marković-Ajanović-Diklić, *Pravopisni priručnik*, Svjetlost, Sarajevo 1975. *Naš jezik u praksi*, Institut za jezik i književnost u Sarajevu, 1979. G. Thomas, *The Role of Lexical Variants in the Present-day Language Situation in Bosnia-Hercegovina*, L.P.L.P, 6:29-44. Cf. also *Bosnie-Herzégovine: littérature et arts en Europe*, Paris, octobre 1979. *Pravopisne teme*, ed. M. Šipka, Sarajevo, Inst. za jezik i književnost, 1980, 390 pp.

134   Cf. Lenin, *Faut-il une langue officielle obligatoire?* Oeuvres, Tome XX, 67-69, Editions sociales, Paris, 1959, Foreign languages editions, Moscow; cf. also V. Lenin, *La question des nationalités ou de l'autonomie*, Oeuvres,

Tome 36, p. 623. Cf. also Lj. Jonke, *Marx, Engels i Lenjin o jeziku*, Vjesnik, 25 October, 1970.

135   Cf. the Parisian daily *Le Monde*, 9 August 1972, p. 3.

136   Cf. B. Banjević, *Jezik i Društvo*, in Stvaranje, Titograd, Sept. 1970. Cf. also the declaration of the Association of Writers of Montenegro: *Ne možemo prihvatiti novosadski dogovor*, Vjesnik, 9 Nov. 1971, p. 3. V. Nikčević, *Čiji je takozvani Vukov jezik*, in Kritika, No. 13, Zagreb, 1970. R. Radojević, *O jeziku i nacionalnoj (ne)ravnopravnosti u teoriji i praksi*, in Kritika, March-April 1969.

137   From Max Weber: *Essays in Sociology*, London, Routlege & Kegan Paul (1970), p. 173.

138   Cf. The New York Times, 27 March 1967, p. 1.

139   S. Babić, B. Finka, M. Moguš, *Hrvatski Pravopis*, London 1972. "The language section of the oldest cultural body in Croatia, Matica hrvatska, initiated work on the Croatian Orthography (*Hrvatski Pravopis*) and laid down the guidelines to be followed in its preparation. These guidelines were examined and approved by other scholarly and professional Croatian institutions, including the Writers' Union of Croatia, the University of Zagreb, the Language Institute of the Yugoslav Academy of Arts and Sciences in Zagreb and the Croatian Philological Association. Three scholars, Dr. Stjepan Babić, Dr. Božidar Finka and Dr. Milan Moguš were put in charge of the project.

By the autumn of 1971, the Croat Orthography was ready for publication. It was expected that it would shortly be approved for use in schools and on mass media. But the sudden dismissal of top political leaders in Croatia, Dr. Savka Dabčević-Kučar and Mika Tripalo, following their dramatic confrontation with President Tito in the army hunting lodge in Karađorđevo on December 1st, produced a change in the situation. A large number of newspapers, magazines and professional journals were banned. The hardest hit of all was *Matica hrvatska*, the most prominent cultural institution in Croatia, all 40,000 copies of the new Orthography, "a mere orthographic rule book" (Dr. Dalibor Brozović) were destroyed. This happened despite the authors' great efforts, evident from their choice of examples in the book, to avoid a head-on clash with the existing political concepts in Yugoslavia. Nevertheless, the new regime called the new book a "nationalist act of sabotage" and ordered legal proceedings against the publishers. (Report of the 28th session of the Central Committee of the Communist Party in Croatia, p. 277) (Preface to Hrvatski Pravopis, p. VI).

140   "This grammar was brought out by the same educational publishing

house in Zagreb that had been responsible for the Orthography in 1972. As soon as the Croatian Grammar had been published in Zagreb in the middle of 1973, it was attacked in the regime press. The main charge was that this handbook for schools 'threatens the brotherhood and unity of the peoples of Yugoslavia' and that it 'causes uneasiness among certain groups'. There were no further explanations, but it was clear that the chief trouble lay in the book's name: Croatian instead of Serbo-Croatian. This was the signal for action against the book which suddenly disappeared from the bookshops. The difference was that this time it was done with less fuss: clearly, the widespread public indignation that followed the destruction of the Orthography 18 months before had taught the authorities a lesson. Hence their rather more discreet handling of the affair.'' The London publishers who reprinted the banned Orthography in 1972 were asked from Croatia to save the Croatian Grammar from total suppression and this language manual was faithfully published in London in October 1974. The controversy over the banning of this grammar is discussed in *Nejezični razgovori o zajedničkom jeziku*, Hrvatska Revija, Munich, 24, No. 4; 482-496.

141   B. Finka, *Trideset godina djelovanja Instituta za jezik JAZU* (1948-1978), in Rasprave Zavoda za jezik, 4-5, 1979, p. 10.

142   Cf. Belgrade weekly NIN 22 June 1980, p. 36, and Zagreb daily Vjesnik, 10 June 1980.

143   Cf. Ch. Spalatin, *Language and Politics in Today's Croatia*, Journal of Croatian Studies, Vol. XX (1979), 2-16. Cf. also Zagreb daily Vjesnik of Dec. 3, 1978.

144   R. Dunatov, ibidem, p. 260.

145   A. Martinet in Preface to *Languages in Contact* by U.   Weinreich, The Hague 1963, p. VIII.

146   R. Dunatov, ibidem, p. 259.   Cf. also S. Babić, *Die Termini für Standard- und Substandard-Idiome im Kroato-serbischen Sprachbereich*, in Zeitschrift für Slavische Philologie XVI, 24-33.

147   The lexical differences between literary Croatian and Serbian affect about ten thousand words in the general vocabulary (common lexicon) and thousands of terms in the scientific and technical vocabularies; eighty-five phenomena of a phonic nature represent the phonetic differences; similarly two hundred cases can be identified concerning word formation and a certain number of ruies of syntax, declension and conjugation which differ in the two languages (see the article by Božidar Vančik in *Bilten Interstena*, Varaždin, No. 2, September, 1967; cf. also T. Ladan, *Centaurski rječnik centaurskog*

jezika, in Kritika 1 (1968), 45-55; J.M. Domenach—A. Pontault, *Yougoslavie*, Seuil, Paris, 1975, p. 7; V. Kalenić, *Lingvostilističko proučavanje hrvatskog jezika*, in Jezik, No. 2-3 (1971-72), 49-63. Lj. Jonke, *Hrvatski književni jezik danas* (The Croatian literary language today), Školska Knjiga, Zagreb, 1971. Idem, *Hrvatski književni jezik 19. i 20. stoljeća* (The Croatian literary language in the 19th and 20th century), Matica hrvatska, Zagreb, 1971. Ch. Spalatin, *Language Situation in Croatia Today*, in Journal of Croatian Studies, Vol. XIV-XV, New York, 1973-74, 3-12. M. Moguš, *Fonološki razvoj hrvatskog jezika* (The Phonological development of the Croatian language), Matica hrvatska, Zagreb, 1971. Rosandić-Silić, *Osnove fonetike i fonologije hrvatskog književnog jezika*, Školska Knjiga, Zagreb, 1974. Id. *Osnove morfologije i morfostilistike hrvatskoga književnog jezika*, Školska Knjiga, Zagreb, 1978. D. Brozović, *O suvremenoj morfološkoj normi hrvatskoga jezičnog standarda i o morfološkim značajkama Standardne novoštokavštine*, in Jezik XXIV (1976-77). D. Brozović, *Deset teza o hrvatskom jeziku*, in Hrvatska Revija, XXV, June 1975, 209-215. Karlo Kosor, *Bilješke o jeziku suvremenih hrvatskih pisaca*, 2 edtion, Split 1979. V. Grubišić, *O hrvatskom jeziku*, Ziral, Rome 1975. Major works are: Z. Vince, *Putovima hrvatskoga književnog jezika*, Sveučilišna naklada Liber, Zagreb, 1978, XIX+629 pp. in -4°. Barić-Lončarić-Malić-Pavešić-Peti-Zečević-Znika, *Priručna gramatika hrvatskoga književnog jezika*, Školska Knjiga, Zagreb, 1979, 527 pp in -4°. An important study is D. Brozović's *Hrvatski jezik, njegovo mjesto unutar južnoslavenskih i drugih slavenskih jezika, njegove povijesne mijene kao jezika hrvatske književnosti*, in Hrvatska književnost u europskom kontekstu, Liber, Zagreb, 1978, 9-75. Cf. also T.F. Magner, *Introduction to the Croatian and Serbian Language*, Philadelphia, Singidunum Press, 1972. M. Engelsfeld, *Croatian Through Conversation*, 4th edition, Zagreb, 1982, 247 pp. V. Barac—Kostrenčić & others, *Let's Learn Croatian*, Stage 1, Center for Foreign Languages, Zagreb, 1982, 278+56 pp.

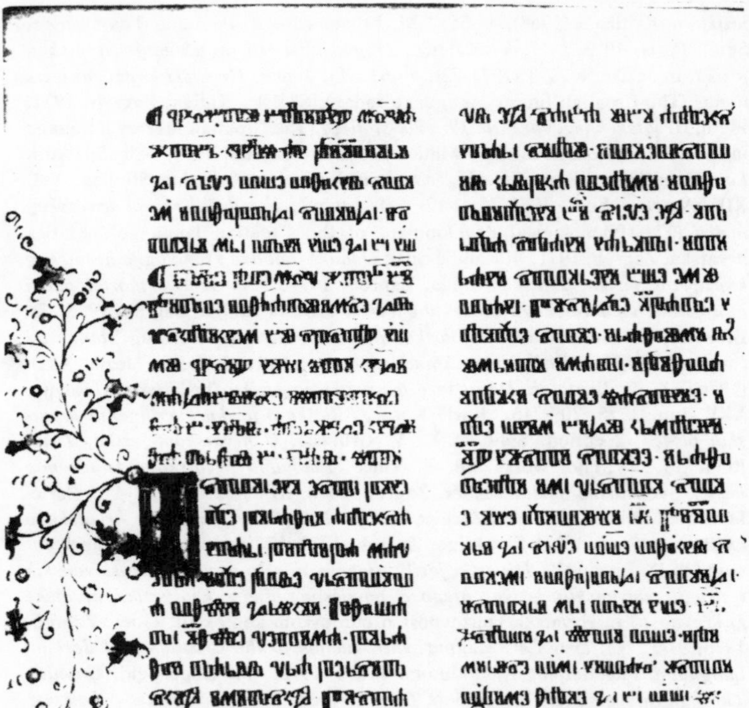

Folio 235ᵛ of the Glagolitic Breviary (1442)

CONTENTS

N° d'éditeur 1191
Dépôt légal. — 4ᵉ trimestre 1984